Guide to
PORCELAINMARKS
of the World

Guide to PORCELAINMARKS of the World

Emanuel Poche

TIGER BOOKS INTERNATIONAL

Designed and produced by
Aventinum Publishers, Prague, Czech Republic
Text by Emanuel Poche
Translated by Joy Moss-Kohoutová
Graphic design by Aleš Krejča

© 1990 AVENTINUM NAKLADATELSTVÍ, s.r.o.

This edition published in 1998 by
Tiger Books International PLC,
Twickenham, UK

ISBN 1-84056-080-0
Printed in the Czech Republic
by Polygrafia, a.s., Prague
2/10/17/51-01

PREFACE

This is intended to be a clear and practical handbook that can be used by anyone interested in porcelain. It is devoted entirely to the factory marks on the ware, and is classified on the basis of the actual appearance of such marks, whether these are objects, words or letters. The reproductions of the marks are accompanied by notes on the location of the factory, the owner or company concerned, the period in which the individual mark was used, and the technique employed in marking the items.

Marks used by modellers or decorators are not included. Such information is sometimes useful, but it would swell this book to cumbersome proportions and cut across any aim of making it a work of reference that the general reader can afford. These artists' marks —which, incidentally, have not yet been brought together in a comprehensive publication —can be gleaned from specialist literature based on the kind of marks given here, which are the most important factors in determining when and where porcelain was made. Only in a few instances, where it helps to describe the ware more precisely, have I included an artist's mark.

In general, I have put on record as many porcelain marks as I possibly could, given the size of the book. Many variants which are similar to one another and come from the same factory — such as different ways of writing the same name —had to be omitted (unless they indicated a different date of origin). On the other hand, I have included marks of English bone china,

5

which is not strictly porcelain. For the uninitiated owner of ceramic products, it is often difficult to decide whether a piece is hard-paste or soft-paste porcelain, or even pottery; the shapes, textures and decorative techniques are often quite similar. By learning the provenance of his possessions through this handbook, the collector should be able to solve this and similar problems.

Porcelain Marks of the World is based on my personal experience — on many years of working to build up the porcelain collection of the Prague Museum of Arts and Crafts, which is one of the biggest in Central Europe. On the basis of my own findings, which agree with those of the outstanding ceramicists, I have put together a book which, hopefully, will prove an efficient guide to its subject.

Emanuel Poche

PORCELAIN MARKS
OF THE WORLD

Porcelain marks are not as old as porcelain itself, but they have been used since the early medieval period. Porcelain was made from the 9th century, if not earlier, and the first great centres of production were the Chinese imperial factories in Kiangsi province (11th century); but the oldest surviving porcelain marks date only from the reign of the Ming emperor Hung Wu (1368—98). For centuries the chief marks on Chinese porcelain were imperial reign marks — appropriately enough in view of the world-wide prestige of porcelain and the absolute power of the Chinese emperor. These reign marks, generally known as *nien hao,* consist of six, or in a few cases four, characters. The characters are arranged in two columns which are always read from top to bottom, beginning with the right-hand column. The two upper right-hand characters indicate the dynasty — until 1643 the Ming, then from 1644 to 1912 the Ch'ing or Manchu dynasty. The third character signifies the family name of the ruling emperor, whose other name is given at the top of the left-hand column. The second character in this column means 'period', and the lowest means 'make' or 'made'.

Sometimes the marks are in a horizontal position, with the name of the dynasty missing; in this instance the marks must be read from right to left. The earliest marks were all inscribed by hand in cobalt under the glaze, but from the beginning of the Ch'ing dynasty there also appear imprints made with seals. These are stylized versions of the characters, being squeezed into a square-shape. However, they can be read off in the same order as other marks.

7

Unlike the marks later used in Europe, Chinese marks are not always reliably dated. The main reason for this was the growing foreign demand for Chinese porcelain, which was particularly noticeable from Ch'ing times. Chinese factories did not hesitate to use the marks of long dead rulers and past years on products intended chiefly for export *(ko huo)*, thus endowing them with a spurious antiquity and rarity value. They even used the old forms of the characters. Spotting such frauds therefore requires long experience and great knowledge of the decorative motifs and colours used on porcelain. Only a few specialists have this, and so it is unlikely that most Chinese porcelain which passes as Ming is really original. Many items are 18th- and 19th-century imitations, including some that were even made abroad — in Japan or Europe — and then given Chinese marks.

The same situation exists with regard to Japanese marked porcelain. The Japanese, however, used various special indications that made it clear that older marks were being imitated.

In addition to the imperial marks on Chinese porcelain there are also sometimes date marks. The dates fall within a sixty year system which the Chinese used as a measure of time in the same way as Europeans use centuries. (The sixty year cycle begins with the year 2637 BC!) Since the porcelain marks do not indicate which sixty year cycle is involved, it must be deduced from the characteristics of the object itself. Where they appear at all, there are always two sixty year cycle marks next to each other.

The place name marks can be a further source of confusion. They give no concrete indication of the locality involved, and even the information they do supply is by no means unambiguous. Sometimes they really indicate the place of production, though in unspecific terms; but quite often what they name is the warehouse from which the porcelain was shipped or the merchant who sold it. There are even instances where these marks represent the buyer of the product, his address and similar details. Such inscriptions often had a kind of poetic significance that was perfectly comprehensible to contemporaries, though it is quite meaningless to us.

Equally lacking in significance now are the so-called dedication marks, representing the names of people who are unidentifiable today. More valuable are advertising marks, which recommend the product through a distinctive and exaggerated poetic terminology; this often contains features that enable the expert to date the object. Very useful, but unfortunately very rare, are the signatures of modellers and decorators. Most of their names mean nothing to modern art historians, but they too indicate a year of production which may at least be the true one. Finally, Chinese porcelain has symbolic marks such as the Eight Buddhist symbols, the Eight Precious Things, and the like.

The marks on Chinese porcelain tell us many things. They reveal, indirectly, the structure of the social system of feudal China. They reveal the complexity of Chinese culture and the Chinese spirit. And above all they reveal the great Chinese love of porcelain, and their pride in it as a creation of their own, famous throughout Asia and Europe. In Europe, from the 14th-century report by Marco Polo to the 'discovery' of its components in Saxony at the beginning of the 18th century, porcelain from China and Japan was regarded as something miraculous and very precious, quite on a par with the other treasures of palaces, churches and the mansions of the wealthy.

The marks used by the other major producer of porcelain in eastern Asia — Japan — are of a different nature. As early as the beginning of the 16th century the Japanese discovered that the secret of making porcelain lay in the use of china clay as the main element, a fact that remained unknown to Europeans for another two hundred years. As well as utilizing the know-ledge, experience and ingenuity of Chinese porcelain makers, the Japanese adopted the Chinese custom of marking, mostly in Chinese characters, the time and place of origin and even the maker. However, the Japanese marks are more straight-forwardly informative than their Chinese counterparts, being laden with none of the allegories and obfuscations dear to the Chinese. In 645 AD the Japanese took over the *nien hao* system of reign marks (called *nengo* in Japanese), but with a different time span. Porcelain products are dated within the framework of these periods, but in view of the fact that until 1873 the Japanese did not use the Gregorian calendar, deciphering these dates is difficult and requires special tables. Furthermore the Japanese too employed the sixty year cycle, but also without properly marking the sequence of the individual periods. (They even imitated the Chinese in dating the cycles back to 2637 BC.) Within each cycle they usually list the individual years, and in view of the scope of this volume it is impossible to discuss these marks in detail. We shall therefore note only those marks that have a concrete content, in other words those that give the place of manufacture (or possibly the maker) and clearly date the product. The Japanese laid much greater stress on such data than the Chinese did. In Japan there was no imperial monopoly, so that there were far more opportunities for business enterprise. Though the marks often carry reminders of 'Great Japan', Japanese porcelain is represented by workshops scattered over almost all the provinces of the empire. The most important were the provinces of Hizen, Kaga and Yamashiro, where the centres of production were the towns of Arita, Kutani and Kyoto, whose porcelain factories created a distinctive style. Their most productive period was the 18th and 19th centuries, when great quantities of porcelain were being exported to Europe. The temptations of the export market often led to the production of pieces that looked older than they really were, and to the imitation of the style in which famous decorators of the past worked.

Japanese porcelain is outstanding for its contrasts of colour. On the one hand there is variety of colours and gilding used to create elaborate painted floral decoration; on the other hand there is the restrained drawing of bamboo shoots and tender leaves. The Japanese strove for a more immediate optical impact than is found in Chinese porcelain, where the aesthetic values are more subtle. The Japanese showed more ingenuity in producing effective decoration, and also made their own technological contribution (cloisonné enamel).

In Europe the marking of porcelain began almost as soon as it was realized that china clay (kaolin) was the main ingredient needed to make true porcelain. This occurred in Saxony at the beginning of the 18th century. However, Europeans had been experimenting for at least a century and a half, and in Italy and France had succeeded in producing versions of soft-paste porcelain. The Medici porcelain of Florence, Saint Cloud ware and other early products were marked, though the object was to record the achievement of the makers rather than to guarantee the authenticity of the objects marked and distinguish them from the wares of competitors.

These motives became important only when Johann Friedrich Böttger, an alchemist in the service of Augustus the Strong, elector of Saxony, discovered how to make hard-paste or true porcelain. The elector hoped to make its manufacture at Meissen, just outside Dresden, a Saxon monopoly, while rulers of neighbouring countries naturally attempted to follow the Saxon example. The first marks used at Meissen were the letters and numbers put on the reverse of each object from 1721; but these were more or less for purposes of registration. Various geometrical marks, incised and painted, were also used, in this case to indicate different types of Oriental porcelain which, for instance, decorated Augustus's Japanese Palace in Dresden.

Böttger's white porcelain was not marked at first; only later did the letters W. R. appear on it. Around 1721 —2 the marking of Meissen porcelain became general practice; the mark used was the so-called Caduceus, which at first resembled Mercury's or Aesculapius' staff. It was used for about ten years, particularly on pieces intended for export. In 1723 another factory mark was introduced, Kite or 'Drachenmarke'.

Apart from these marks, which gave no specific indication of provenance, a mark giving the place of origin was introduced in 1722: the letters M.P.M. (Meissner Porzellanmanufaktur) or K.P.M. (Königliche Porzellanmanufaktur), which were however employed only on pots and sugar basins. A year later a mark was adopted which is used to this day and has become world famous: crossed swords (taken from the coat of arms of Saxony), at first combined with the mark K.P.M. From 1724 the crossed swords mark was used on its own (though it was not officially introduced until 1731), and to this day it is the exclusive mark of Meissen production. At the outset the crossed swords were impressed, but later they were painted in cobalt blue under the glaze, as they have been ever since. Over the centuries the actual drawing of this mark has undergone several alterations. Other marks were also sometimes added, and these often gave their names to the periods in question. Thus during the dot period a dot was placed between the cross-guards of the swords; the term applies to the period 1763—80 although, as Rückert has pointed out, the dot occasionally appeared as early as the 1730's. The same is true of the star between the sword hilts, which gave its name to the star period, when the factory was managed by Count Camillo Marcolini (1774—1814); in this period there were still other additional marks, from which it is possible to deduce the names of the heads of the painting workshop. From the 1760's the quality of inferior items was indicated by incised lines crossing the mark once, twice or three times over or under the swords. Porcelain ordered for the king and his court between 1723 and 1736 carried the monogram AR (Augustus Rex). Special marks were also made on porcelain manufactured for the Saxon court in Dresden and in Warsaw (Augustus being king of Poland as well as elector of Saxony).

Apart from factory marks, some products of the 1730's carried impressed marks made by the modeller; then, in 1740, modellers' marks were replaced by numerals. Finally, the numbering of models, carried out retrospectively in 1749 when the manufacture was directed by J. J. Kändler, added to the difficulty of deciphering Meissen markings. Such was the productivity of Meissen that by 1764 no less than 3051 models had been registered.

The crossed swords mark is the oldest European porcelain mark that is still in use. It symbolizes an output which, in the 18th century, and particularly thanks to J.J. Kändler, achieved the status of high art. As such it had a tremendous influence on contemporary culture, of which it gives us an especially vivid picture.

It is interesting that Meissen's closest competitor, the factory in imperial Vienna, left its products unmarked for nearly three decades. This can hardly be explained by the involvement of private enterprise in the person of Claudius Innocentius du Paquier, since the Berlin entrepreneur Wegely marked his ware with his own monogram. Apparently du Paquier did not mark ware from his factory for the simple reason that it was not yet custom in 1718, when he started production.

Viennese porcelain began to be marked only when the factory was bought by the state in 1744. The mark chosen was the emblem of the duchy of Austria, a heraldic shield with a beam across it. Its shape gave rise to the erroneous belief that it was intended to represent a beehive. The Viennese imperial porcelain factory employed this mark, which was first impressed, then painted, and later still impressed again, for more than a hundred years, until the factory closed in 1864.

As well as the factory mark, Vienna porcelain carried complicated subsidiary markings which provided information about the maker and the date of production. In the 18th century porcelain figures carried modellers' marks in the form of various impressed letters; in the 19th century the presence of painted numerals provided information about several

12

generations of painters of all genres —figure painters and decorative painters, and painters of landscapes and still-lifes. The factory also indicated the year of production with impressed numbers; and the practice was copied by several other porcelain factories in the Austro-Hungarian Empire, including the Czech factories at Slavkov and Klášterec nad Ohří.

With the expansion of porcelain production in the German states and throughout Europe in the later 18th century, marking systems became the rule. Royal and aristocratic entrepreneurs, stimulated by the achievements of the factories at Meissen, Vienna and Venice, vied with one another in setting up their own concerns, and in the process developed a number of systems of marking porcelain. The two Ls monogram of Louis XV appeared on Sèvres porcelain, and in the 18th and 19th centuries the monograms of various monarchs, shown with a crown, were commonly seen. But an even more popular way of marking porcelain in the 19th century was to use a symbolic motif. The symbol of the state or ruler was shown through some heraldic device (a coat of arms, or certain elements of one, or else the ruler's insignia), often followed by a symbol representing the place of production. In addition to the heraldic marks already mentioned, there are those of St Petersburg, Nymphenburg and Herend, and of Italian and Spanish porcelain. In the second category it is possible to include the silhouette of the dome of Florence Cathedral on Medici porcelain, as well as the motif of the sea on Copenhagen porcelain; and there are a good many others.

With the further expansion of porcelain production in the 19th century, the period of the industrial revolution, hundreds and hundreds of new porcelain factories sprang up. The resulting fierce competition, haste and mechanization of production did not encourage painstaking differentiation between marks by means of symbols. It became the practice for a firm to follow the English example and simply give its name, either in full or in abbreviated form, which sufficiently indicated the locality and/or ownership of the company. The symbol, where it was still used, became at best a minor decorative motif. There were fewer hand-written marks, and with the introduction of copperplate printing on porcelain (also based on the English model) printed marks made with a stamp became commonplace. But the desire for profit or the need to survive sometimes came into conflict with the principle of correct marking. In such cases, marks were altered so as to resemble the symbols or monograms of the factories manufacturing the best wares. This tendency had been in evidence from the earliest days of European porcelain; at Meissen, for example, Böttger's products had been inscribed with Oriental, usually Chinese, characters and symbols. Similarly, 18th-century English businessmen at Derby, Worcester and Caughley did not hesitate to use quasi-Oriental marks, tacitly claiming that their ware was comparable in quality to Oriental porcelain. These earlier practices concealed no fraudulent intentions; they were, rather, an expression of admiration and respect for centuries of Oriental tradition, as well as representing an attempt to exploit its popularity. In the 19th century, practices of this sort were less innocent in intention. Many marks were intended to create the impression that the ware had been produced at one of the great European centres. The Meissen mark was imitated in England (at Chelsea, Derby, Worcester and Bristol), in Belgium (at Tournai), in Holland (at Weesp), and in Germany itself at such factories as Rauenstein, Limbach, Nymphenburg, Volkstedt and Wallendorf. In Bohemia the Loket and Dubí factories imitated Meissen; and as far away as Russia the Englishman Francis Gardner did the same at Verbilki. Sèvres porcelain, with its world-wide reputation, also proved a magnet for imitators, who copied the famous intertwined Ls; among the imitators were the factories at Valenciennes, Limoges and Foëcy in France, Derby and Worcester in England, and several lesser known porcelain factories in Germany. The mark of the imperial factory in Vienna was imitated too, but not so blatantly as the Sèvres and Meissen marks—probably because the Viennese factory was gradually declining in importance. But a modern firm that has complicated the identification of Viennese porcelain is the Vienna-Augarten, which since 1922 has been manufacturing ware in modern styles, but has also produced historicizing porcelain, including tableware with subjects taken from the Neo-Classical Sorgenthal period.

The leading factories naturally did their best to protect themselves against imitation of their marks, even if only a general similarity was involved. The effectiveness of such imitations was thus often ephemeral. Yet such forgeries and imitations have managed to deceive experienced collectors and the curators of museum collections, and it has therefore become necessary to devote increased attention to marks and to assess them in the context of the overall character of the object concerned. In trying to discover where and when it was made, the basic criterion is always the nature of the material used. In certain cases this can be an absolutely decisive consideration. For example, some porcelain factories have disposed of — still dispose of —original models from which new casts can be taken again and again. Superficially there may be no way of telling whether an object is two years or two hundred years old. This is most notoriously true of Meissen, but it also applies to Höchst, whose models were taken over by the factory at Damm, which even used the same mark as Höchst. This, however, was merely an episode around 1800, whereas Meissen 'Rococo porcelain' is manufactured to this day with 18th-century lavishness and superb technique. The Berlin factory too has made new casts from 18th-century models. However, since the 19th century Berlin has used different marks for its products, including casts made from 18th-century models; so there is no difficulty in distinguishing between the old and the new.

Where the mark is the same, detailed examination will generally show up the differences. The body of a modern cast is usually smooth and unbroken; for instance the bases of the figures are not cracked. The glaze is brilliant and shiny, and the tones of the colours often differ from those of the 18th-century palette. This is particularly true of the countless idyllic Rococo-like figures and groups which, thanks to their decorative charm, remain enormously popular with the public at large.

Modern copies of tableware are even easier to spot. Copyists make all sorts of mistakes as to both the shape of the ware — overemphasizing its 'period' features —and its painted decoration. Modern decorators are never as successful as their 18th- and early 19th-century predecessors in creating Rococo and Neo-Classical subjects such as flowers, landscapes, figures and scenes. In particular, they find it impossible to simulate the brushwork of the old painters. Even in China and Japan, where imitating ancient models was a traditional occupation (pursued with such success by the 18th century that the results were often indistinguishable from the originals), the craft declined in the 19th century. Here too the copy is always given away by the brushstrokes, the subject matter, or the composition of the materials employed.

It should be clear from all this that the authenticity of marks must always be verified. The mark must be examined with the character of the object itself in mind, and all the more so since porcelain is perhaps the only art in which historicism is still alive today. Deliberate forgeries apart, there is a continuing popular demand for pseudo-Rococo tableware and modern 'kitch' reproductions of the Empire style. Porcelain lends itself perfectly to Rococo and Neo-Classicism, with the result that these have become the accepted styles for any artistic work in the medium. Only modern utility porcelain, and some decorative porcelain produced by outstanding artists at such factories as Sèvres, Copenhagen, Ludwigsburg and Meissen, have broken with tradition and struck any kind of modern note.

And this may change in the future. For although this once precious material has become a daily commonplace, its qualities are such that it is unlikely ever to be replaced by some modern synthetic material.

MARKS

NOTE ON THE CLASSIFICATION
OF MARKS

The marks in this book are grouped according to their subject matter. This seemed the arrangement best suited to the practical needs of readers, for whom the factory mark of an object is the chief and most reliable indication of when, where and by whom it was made. One group here consists of marks whose main motifs are pictorial symbols, in another and much larger group the main features are place names, or the names or monograms of the producers. However, it is a very difficult matter to classify all the marks so unambiguously since some of them are composed of more than one symbol. In such cases the author could only decide for himself to which group a particular mark belonged. For this reason, when readers are investigating a mark they should check up on all the motifs to be found on it.

The sequence of groups is as follows: the sun 1—7; the moon 8—19; the stars 20—30; water 31—3; flora 34—79; man and parts of his body 80—87; fauna 88—122; insignia and heraldic devices 123—234; emblems 235—6; 'Zachen-balken' 237—8; arms 239—55; implements, instruments and machines 256—313; buildings 314—28; symbols and geometric motifs 329—59; Roman alphabet marks 360—1738; Cyrillic alphabet marks 1739—1801; Oriental marks 1802— —2031; European imitations of Oriental marks 2032—2061.

LIST OF ABBREVIATIONS

A	Austria
B	Belgium
CH	Switzerland
CZ	Czech Republic
D	Germany
DK	Denmark
E	Spain
F	France
FIN	Finland
GB	Great Britain
H	Hungary
I	Italy
IRL	Ireland
J	Japan
L	Luxembourg
LV	Latvia
NL	Netherlands
P	Portugal
PL	Poland
RO	Romania
RUS	Russia
S	Sweden
UA	Ukraine
YU	Yugoslavia

#		
1		SAINT CLOUD Royal Porcelain Factory 1693—1722 / *blue*
2		SAINT CLOUD Royal Porcelain Factory 1693—1722 / *blue*
3		SAINT CLOUD Royal Porcelain Factory 1693—1722 / *blue*
4		VOLKSTEDT-RUDOLSTADT H. Greiner 1808—1870 / *blue*
5		LICHTE Heubach Bros 19th cent. / *printed*
6		TURN (Trnovany) Riessner & Kessel, "Amphora" from 1892 / *printed*
7		SCHIRNDING Porzellanfabrik from 1902 / *printed*
8		BOW W. Duesbury 1762—1776 / *blue*
9		WORCESTER Dr Wall 1751—1783 / *blue*
10		WORCESTER Dr Wall 1751—1783 / *red*

11	**WORCESTER** Dr Wall 1751—1783 / *red*
12	**LOWESTOFT** imitations of Worcester 2nd half of 18th cent. / *blue*
13 **14**	**CAUGHLEY** T. Turner 1772—1799 / *blue*
15 **16**	**CAUGHLEY** T. Turner 1772—1799 / *blue*
17	**PINXTON** W. Billingsley 1796—1813 / *red*
18	**COPENHAGEN** Royal Porcelain Factory 19th cent. / *impressed*
19	**OESLAU** W. Goebel from 1879 / *printed*
20	**DOCCIA** L. Ginori 1770—1790 / *red*
21	**DOCCIA** C. L. Ginori late 18th—early 19th cent. *blue, red, gold*
22 **23** **24**	**DOCCIA** C. L. Ginori late 18th —early 19th cent. / *blue*
25	**DOCCIA** Ginori late 19th cent. / *impressed*
26 **27**	**LE NOVE** E. P. Antonibon from 1763 / *red, gold* / *blue, red, gold*

28		LONGTON Paragon China Ltd. from 1919 / *printed*
29	 	NOVGOROD Kuznetsov 1st half of 19th cent. / *blue*
30		TOMASZOW M. Mezer 1806—1810 / *printed*
31		COPENHAGEN Royal Porcelain Factory 1830—1845 / *blue*
32		COPENHAGEN Royal Porcelain Factory 1830—1845 / *blue*
33		COPENHAGEN Royal Porcelain Factory 1830—1845 / *blue*
34		SCHLAGGENWALD (Slavkov) Haas & Czjizek 1888—1906 / *printed*
35		SCHLAGGENWALD (Slavkov) Haas & Czjizek 20th cent. / *printed*
36		SCHLAGGENWALD (Slavkov) Haas & Czjizek 1888—1896 / *printed*
37		CHODAU (Chodov) Haas & Czjizek from 1905 / *printed*

38		WALDENBURG (Walbrzych) Krister Porzellanmanufaktur 1831—1943 / *blue*
39		REHAU Zeh, Scherzer & Co. from 1880 / *printed*
40		CAPODIMONTE Royal Porcelain Factory 1743—1759 / *impressed*
41		PARIS, PONT AUX CHOUX "Mignon" 1777—1784 / *blue*
42		SAINT CLOUD Royal Porcelain Factory 1696 / *incised*
43 44		PARIS, PONT AUX CHOUX "Mignon" 1777—1784 / *blue*
45 46		CAPODIMONTE Royal Porcelain Factory 1743—1759 / *blue*
47		BUEN RETIRO Royal Porcelain Factory 1760—1803 / *blue*
48		CAPODIMONTE Royal Porcelain Factory 1743—1759 / *blue*
49 50 51		BUEN RETIRO Royal Porcelain Factory 1760—1803 / *blue*
52		BUEN RETIRO Royal Porcelain Factory 1760—1803 / *blue*

53		CHELSEA N. Sprimont & C. Gouyn 1745—1749 / *blue*
54		LIMBACH G. Greiner after 1787 / *red, green, gold, black*
55 56		KLOSTER VEILSDORF G. Greiner 1797—1822 / *blue*
57		ORLÉANS Manufacture Royale after 1753(?) or after 1766 / *blue*
58		PARIS, RUE DE LA ROQUETTE Souroux after 1773 / *blue, red*
59	J. S. GERMANY	CHARLOTTENBRUNN (Zofiówka) J. Schachtel after 1859 / *printed*
60	M	ALT-ROHLAU (Stará Role) M. Zdekauer after 1881 / *printed*
61		NIEDERSALZBRUNN (Szczawienko) H. Ohme after 1882 / *printed*
62	R C W	WUNSIEDEL Retsch & Co. after 1885 / *printed*
63	BAVARIA	WUNSIEDEL Retsch & Co. after 1885 / *printed*

64		COALPORT J. Rose after 1796 / *printed*
65		MERKELSGRÜN (Merklin) 1881—1918 / *printed*
66		MARKTREDWITZ Jaeger & Co. after 1872 / *printed*
67		SCHAALA H. Voigt after 1872 / *printed*
68		POTSCHAPPEL C. Thieme after 1872 / *printed*
69		LICHTE Heubach Bros after 1820 / *blue*
70		PLAUE C. G. Schierholz & Sohn after 1817 / *blue*
71		PLAUE C. G. Schierholz & Sohn after 1817 / *printed*
72		PLAUE C. G. Schierholz & Sohn after 1817 / *printed*

73		GROSSBREITENBACH G. Greiner after 1783 / *blue*
74		LIMBACH G. Greiner after 1787 / *blue*
75		ILMENAU G. Greiner 1787—1792 / *blue*
76		LIMBACH Porcelain Factory middle of 19th cent. *printed*
77		GROSSBREITENBACH H. Bühl & Söhne 19th cent. / *printed*
78		DUX (Duchcov) E. Eichler after 1860 / *printed*
79		GEHREN J. Günthersfeld & Co. after 1884 / *printed*
80		MILAN San Cristoforo after 1945 / *printed*
81		VIENNA, WILHELMSBURG Oest. Keramik A. G. 1883—1945 / *printed*

82		OHRDRUF Baehr & Proeschild after 1871 / *printed*
83		ELBOGEN (Loket) R. & F. Haidinger 1815—1833 / *blue*
84		ELBOGEN (Loket) R. & F. Haidinger 1833—1860 / *impressed*
85		ELBOGEN (Loket) Springer & Co. *c.* 1900 / *blue*
86		ELBOGEN (Loket) "Epiag" 1938—1945 / *blue*
87		POSSNECK Conta & Böhme after 1790 / *blue*
88		KASSEL Friedrich II of Hesse-Kassel 1766—1788 / *blue*
89		FRANKENTHAL J. A. Hannong 1756—1759 / *blue*
90		MARKTSCHWABEN Keramische Fabrik 19th cent. / *printed*

91		HEREND Porcelain Factory 1897 / *printed*
92		TETTAU G. C. Greiner after 1885 / *gold*
93	 	SWINTON Royal Rockingham Works 1820—1842 / *printed*
94		FÜRSTENBERG Fürstliche Porzellanmanufactur 1770—1814 / *impressed*
95	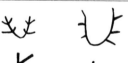	UNTERWEISSBACH Mann & Porzelius A. G. 19th cent. / *printed*
96		KLÖSTERLE (Klášterec) M. Weber 1796—1803 / *red, black*
97 98		KLÖSTERLE (Klášterec) M. Weber 1804—1830 / *blue, various colours*
99		LUDWIGSBURG Carl Eugen of Württemberg 1759—1806 / *blue*
100		LUDWIGSBURG Carl Eugen of Württemberg 1759—1806 / *blue*

101		LUDWIGSBURG Carl Eugen of Württemberg 1759—1806 / *blue*
102		KATZHÜTTE Hertwig & Co. 19th cent. until 1945 / *impressed*
103 104		HAGUE A. & J. F. Lynker 1776—1790 / *blue*
105		HAGUE A. & J. F. Lynker 1776—1790 / *blue*
106		HAGUE A. & J. F. Lynker 1776—1790 / *blue*
107		SUHL E. Schlegelmilch after 1861 / *printed*
108		VIENNA, WILHELMSBURG Oest. Keramik A. G. 1883—1945 / *printed*
109		FENTON E. Brain & Co. after 1900 / *printed*
110		BARCELONA Manufacturas Cerámicas after 1921 / *printed*

111		MARKTREDWITZ Jaeger & Co. after 1872 / *printed*
112	 	ANSBACH Markgräfliche Porzellan- manufaktur 1758—1790 / *blue*
113		ANSBACH Markgräfliche Porzellan- manufaktur 1758—1790 / *blue*
114 **115**		NYON J. Dortu & F. Müller 1781—1813 / *blue*
116		KÖPPELSDORF J. Hering & Sohn after 1893 / *printed*
117		LILLE Leperre-Durot 1784—1817 / *red*
118		LILLE Leperre-Durot 1784—1817 / *red*
119		MITTERTEICH M. Emanuel & Co. after 1900 / *printed*

120		OESLAU W. Goebel after 1879 / *printed*
121		EICHWALD (Dubí) Bloch & Co. after 1871 / *blue*
122		POSTSCHAPPEL C. Thieme after 1872 / *blue*
123		MARIEBERG P. Berthevin 1777—1778 / *red, blue*
124		MARIEBERG P. Berthevin 1777—1778 / *red, blue*
125		RÖRSTRAND B. R. Geyer beginning of 19th cent. / *blue* *gold*
126		EICHWALD (Dubí) Bloch & Co. after 1871 / *blue*
127		LANGEWIESEN O. Schlegelmilch after 1872 / *blue*
128		HILDESHEIM after 1760 / *blue*

129		BUEN RETIRO Charles III of Spain after 1759 / *blue*
130		DERBY Crown Porcelain Co. 1877—1889 / *printed*
131		DERBY Crown Porcelain Co. after 1890 / *printed*
132		DERBY Crown Porcelain Co. 1784—1811 / *gold*
133		BOCK-WALLENDORF Fasold & Stauch after 1903 / *printed*
134		WORCESTER Royal Worcester Porcelain Co. from 1862 / *printed*
135		FENTON Crown Staffordshire China after 1801 / *printed*
136		FISCHERN (Rybáře) C. Knoll beginning of 20th cent. / *printed*

137		WALDENBURG (Walbrzych) C. Tielsch 2nd half of 19th cent. / *blue*
138		PIRKENHAMMER (Březová) after 1890 until 1938 / *red,* *printed*
139		COPENHAGEN Royal Porcelain Factory 1905 / *gold*
140		COPENHAGEN Royal Porcelain Factory 1905 / *gold*
141		COPENHAGEN Royal Porcelain Factory from 1929 / *gold*
142		KAHLA Porcelain Factory after 1844 / *printed*
143		ELLWANGEN A. F. Prahl's widow *c.* 1760 / *blue*
144		ELLWANGEN A. F. Prahl's widow *c.* 1760 / *blue*

145		**HELSINKI** Arabia A/B 1874—1917 / *printed*
146		**HEREND** Porcelain Factory *c.* 1850 / *blue*
147		**HEREND** Porcelain Factory 1900—1934 / *blue*
148		**HEREND** Porcelain Factory 1891—1897 / *blue*
149		**FRYAZINO** Barmin Bros 1820—1850 / *blue*
150		**HOHENBERG** C. M. Hutschenreuther 1865 / *printed*
151		**BADEN-BADEN** Z. Pfalzer 1771—1778 / *blue*
152		**SAARGEMÜND** Utzschneider & Co. 19th cent. / *printed*

153	 	SAARGEMÜND Utzschneider & Co. 19th cent. / *printed*
154		TURN (Trnovany) E. Wahliss, "Alexandra- Porcelain-Works" after 1894 / *printed*
155 **156**		TIRSCHENREUTH Porzellanfabrik 2nd half of 19th cent. / *printed*
157		TURN (Trnovany) E. Wahliss, "Alexandra- Porcelain-Works" after 1894 / *printed*
158		HELSINKI Arabia A/B after 1874 / *printed*
159 **160**		REHAU Zeh, Scherzer & Co. *c.* 1900 / *printed*
161		ANSBACH Markgräfliche Porzellan- manufaktur last quarter of 18th cent. *impressed*
162		ANSBACH Markgräfliche Porzellan- manufaktur *c.* 1765 and 19th cent. / *blue*

163		ANSBACH Markgräfliche Porzellan- manufaktur c. 1765 and 19th cent. / *blue*
164		VIENNA Staatsmanufaktur 2nd half of 18th cent. / *blue*
165		VIENNA Staatsmanufaktur 1744—1749 / *incised*
166		VIENNA Staatsmanufaktur 1749—1820 / *blue*
167		VIENNA Staatsmanufaktur 1744—1749 / *impressed*
168		VIENNA Staatsmanufaktur 1820—1827 / *blue*
169		VIENNA Staatsmanufaktur 1760—1770 / *blue*
170 **171**		NYMPHENBURG Kurfürstliche Porzellan- manufaktur 1755—1765 / *impressed*
172		NYMPHENBURG Kurfürstliche Porzellan- manufaktur 1810—1850 / *impressed*
173		NYMPHENBURG Kurfürstliche Porzellan- manufaktur 1780—1790 / *impressed*
174		NYMPHENBURG Kurfürstliche Porzellan- manufaktur 1850—1862 / *impressed*

175 176		FRANKENTHAL P. Hannong 1755—1759 / *blue*
177		BLANKENHAIN C. & A. Carstens 19th cent. / *blue*
178		PIRKENHAMMER (Březová) Fischer & Mieg after 1887—1890 / *gold*
179 180 181		BERLIN Königliche Porzellanmanufaktur 1763—1780 / *blue*
182 183		BERLIN Königliche Porzellanmanufaktur 1780—1880 / *blue*
184		BERLIN Königliche Porzellanmanufaktur 1875—1944 / *blue*
185		BERLIN Königliche Porzellanmanufaktur 1847—1849 / *printed*
186		BERLIN Königliche Porzellanmanufaktur 1849—1870 / *printed*

187		PASSAU Dressel, Kister & Co. 2nd half of 19th cent. / *blue*
188		MEISSEN Böttger stoneware 1707—1720 / *impressed*
189		MEISSEN J. F. Böttger 1710—1720 / *blue*
190		MEISSEN Königliche Porzellanmanufaktur 1725—1730 / *blue*
191		MEISSEN Königliche Porzellanmanufaktur 1730 / *blue*
192		MEISSEN Königliche Porzellanmanufaktur 1731 / *blue*
193		MEISSEN Königliche Porzellanmanufaktur 1723—1724 / *blue*
194 195		MEISSEN Königliche Porzellanmanufaktur 1725—1730 / *blue*
196		MEISSEN Königliche Porzellanmanufaktur 1725—1730 / *blue*

197	MEISSEN Königliche Porzellanmanufaktur 1730—1735 / *blue*
198	MEISSEN Königliche Porzellanmanufaktur 1730—1740 / *blue*
199	MEISSEN Königliche Porzellanmanufaktur after 1750 / *blue*
200	MEISSEN Königliche Porzellanmanufaktur 1730—1740 / *blue*
201	MEISSEN Königliche Porzellanmanufaktur *c.* 1765 / *blue*
202 203	MEISSEN Königliche Porzellanmanufaktur after 1763 / *blue*
204 205	MEISSEN Königliche Porzellanmanufaktur after 1774 / *blue*
206	MEISSEN Königliche Porzellanmanufaktur 1772 and after 1774 / *blue*
207	MEISSEN Königliche Porzellanmanufaktur 1774—1830 / *impressed*

208		MEISSEN Königliche Porzellanmanufaktur beginning of 19th cent. / *blue*
209		MEISSEN Königliche Porzellanmanufaktur after 1723, with mark of Master Kretschner added / *blue*
210		MEISSEN Königliche Porzellanmanufaktur 1st half of 18th cent., with mark of Master Moebius / *blue*
211		MEISSEN Königliche Porzellanmanufaktur after 1766, medium quality *blue*
212		MEISSEN Königliche Porzellanmanufaktur after 1766, medium quality, unpainted / *blue*
213		MEISSEN Königliche Porzellanmanufaktur after 1766, medium quality, painted / *blue*
214		MEISSEN Königliche Porzellanmanufaktur after 1766, discarded, painted / *blue*
215		MEISSEN Königliche Porzellanmanufaktur after 1766, discarded, unpainted / *blue*
216		MEISSEN Königliche Porzellanmanufaktur after 1766, second quality, painted / *blue*
217		MEISSEN Königliche Porzellanmanufaktur after 1766, third quality / *blue*

218		MEISSEN Königliche Porzellanmanufaktur after 1766, discarded / *blue*
219		MEISSEN Königliche Hofconditorei Warschau 1763—1806 / *black, red*
220		MEISSEN Königliche Porzellanmanufaktur after 1724, with a number indicating the service / *blue*
221		MEISSEN Königliche Porzellanmanufaktur modellers' marks, 18th cent. *blue* Georg Kittel Peter Geithner Gottfried Lohse Johann Christoph Krumbholtz Johann Donner Johann Kittel Christoph Busch Johann Meisel Georg Michel Johann Michal Schuhmann
222		VOLKSTEDT-RUDOLSTADT C. Nonne after 1788—1799 / *blue*
223		LOWESTOFT imitation of Meissen mark 18th cent. / *blue*
224		CHELSEA imitations of Meissen 18th cent. / *blue, gold*
225		WEESP Count Gronsveldt-Diepenbroek 1759—1771 / *blue*

226		WEESP Count Gronsveldt-Diepenbroek 1759—1771 / *blue*
227		BRISTOL R. Champion end of 18th cent. / *blue, incised*
228		BRISTOL R. Champion end of 18th cent. / *blue, incised*
229		BRISTOL R. Champion end of 18th cent. / *blue, incised*
230		BRISTOL R. Champion end of 18th cent. / *blue, incised*
231		BRISTOL R. Champion 1773—1781 / *blue, incised*
232		WORCESTER Dr Wall 1751—1783 / *blue*
233		DERBY imitations of Meissen middle of 18th cent. / *blue*
234		TOURNAI F. J. Peterinck 1763—1800 / *blue, gold*

235		KÖPPELSDORF J. Hering & Sohn c. 1893 / *printed*
236		FREIWALDAU (Gozdnica) H. Schmidt 2nd half of 19th cent. / *printed*
237		VINCENNES Séguin factory, coat of arms of the duke of Chartres after 1777—1788 / *blue*
238		ORLÉANS Manufacture Royale de porce- layne d'Orléans 1767—1806 / *blue*
239		PARIS, RUE DE LA ROQUETTE J. V. Dubois after 1774 / *blue*
240		EISENBERG Porzellanfabrik Kalk G. m. b. H. after 1900 / *blue*
241		MITTERTEICH M. Emanuel & Co. after 1900 / *printed*
242		BOW Weatherby & Crowther c. 1750 / *blue*
243		WORCESTER Wall period 1751—1783 / *blue*
244		BOW Weatherby & Crowther c. 1750 / *incised*

245	GIESSHÜBEL (Kysibl) C. Nonne & K. Roesch 1803—1811 / *blue*
246	GIESSHÜBEL (Kysibl) B. Knaute 1815—1828 / *blue*
247 **248**	GIESSHÜBEL (Kysibl) B. Knaute 1828—1830 / *blue*
249	PARIS, RUE DE LA ROQUETTE F. Hébert 1741—1752 / *blue*
250	GRÄFENTHAL Unger, Schneider, Hutschen- reuther & Co. after 1861 / *blue*
251 **252** **253**	GRÄFENTHAL Unger, Schneider, Hutschen- reuther & Co. after 1861 / *blue*
254	PARIS, RUE DE LA ROQUETTE J. V. Dubois after 1774 / *blue*
255	MITTERTEICH M. Emanuel & Co. after 1900 / *printed*

256		CHELSEA Triangle period (Sprimont- Gouyn) 1745—1750 / *blue*
257 258		PARIS, RUE FONTAINE AU ROY L. Russinger after 1771 / *blue*
259		PARIS, RUE FONTAINE AU ROY Pouyat after 1800 / *blue*
260 261		VOLKSTEDT-RUDOLSTADT C. Nonne 1787—1799 / *blue*
262		VOLKSTEDT-RUDOLSTADT C. Nonne 1808—1890 / *blue*
263		VOLKSTEDT-RUDOLSTADT C. Nonne 1808—1890 / *blue*
264 265		VOLKSTEDT-RUDOLSTADT R. Eckert & Co. after 1895—after 1900 *printed*
266		VOLKSTEDT-RUDOLSTADT R. Eckert & Co. after 1895—after 1900 / *printed*
267 268		PARIS, FAUBOURG SAINT DENIS Pierre A. Hannong 1771—1776 / *blue*
269		KÖPPELSDORF-NORD Schoenau Bros, Swaine & Co. after 1854 / *blue*

270 271	**ARNSTADT** Porzellanfabrik after 1790 / *blue*
272	**SCEAUX** J. Jullien & S. Jacques 1763—1772 / *incised*
273 274	**VENICE** G. Cozzi 1766—1813 / *red, gold*
275	**CHELSEA** Anchor period (Sprimont-Fawkener) after 1753—1758 / *red*
276	**CHELSEA** Anchor period (Sprimont-Fawkener) after 1753—1758 / *blue*
277	**CHELSEA** Anchor period (Sprimont-Fawkener) after 1750—1753 / *red*
278	**BOW** W. Duesbury 1760—1766 / *red*
279 280	**SCHWARZENBACH** O. Schaller & Co. after 1882 / *printed*
281	**BARANOVKA** Mezer Bros 1804—1850 / *blue*
282	**BOW** W. Duesbury 1760—1776 / *red*
283	**BOW** W. Duesbury 1760—1776 / *blue, red*
284	**BOW** W. Duesbury 1760—1776 / *red*

285		BOW W. Duesbury 1760—1776 / *red*
286		CHELSEA Raised Anchor period 1750—1753 / *impressed*
287		HÖCHST Kurfürstliche Porzellan- manufaktur 1758—1765 / *impressed*
288 289		HÖCHST Kurfürstliche Porzellan- manufaktur 1750—1763 / *red, black, brown* / *blue*
290		HÖCHST Kurfürst Emmerich von Breiden- bach 1765—1774 / *blue*
291		PASSAU imitations of Höchst 19th cent. / *blue*
292 293		DAMM casts from Höchst's models 1860—1888 / *blue*
294		DAMM casts from Höchst's models 1840—1845 / *blue*
295		DAMM casts from Höchst's models 1850—1860 / *blue*
296		DAMM casts from Höchst's models 19th cent. / *blue*

297		CHANTILLY Prince de Condé 1726—1740 / *blue, red*
298		CHANTILLY Prince de Condé 1740—1800 / *blue*
299		CHANTILLY Prince de Condé 1740—1800 / *blue*
300		ALT-ROHLAU (Stará Role) F. Manka from 1883 / *printed*
301		OHRDRUF Kling & Co. 1836—1941 / *printed*
302		VIENNA M. G. Grossbaum 1889 / *blue*
303		ALT-HALDENSLEBEN Schmerzer & Gericke 2nd half of 19th cent. / *printed*
304		ALT-ROHLAU (Stará Role) M. Zdekauer after 1884 / *printed*
305		DELFT Ary de Milde end of 17th cent. / *impressed*

306		LORCH Deusch & Co. after 1898 / *printed*
307		MITTERTEICH M. Emanuel & Co. end of 19th cent. / *printed*
308		ILMENAU Metzler Bros & Ortloff after 1876 / *printed*
309		SCHEDEWITZ A. Unger 20th cent. / *printed*
310		STADTLENGSFELD Porzellanfabrik A. G. *c.* 1900 / *printed*
311		DOCCIA R. Ginori 18th cent. / *blue*
312		KÖPPELSDORF E. Heubach after 1887 / *blue*
313		STADTLENGSFELD Porzellanfabrik A. G. *c.* 1920 / *printed*

314		TOURNAI F. J. Peterinck 1753—1780 / *blue, gold*
315		TOURNAI F. J. Peterinck 1753—1780 / *gold*
316		TOURNAI F. J. Peterinck 1753—1780 / *red, violet*
317		TOURNAI F. J. Peterinck 1753—1780 / *gold*
318		TOURNAI F. J. Peterinck 1752—1762 / *various colours*
319 320		TOURNAI F. J. Peterinck 1752—1762 / *various colours*
321		TOURNAI F. J. Peterinck 1752—1762 / *various colours*
322		PARIS, CLIGNANCOURT P. Deruelle after 1771—1775 / *gold*
323		PARIS, CLIGNANCOURT P. Deruelle after 1771—1775 / *red*
324		MANTUA, CANETTO SULL'OGLIO Ceramica Furga after 1872 / *printed*

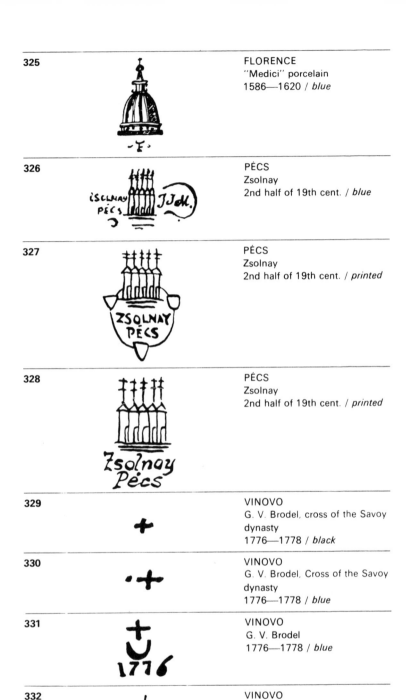

325		FLORENCE "Medici" porcelain 1586—1620 / *blue*
326		PÉCS Zsolnay 2nd half of 19th cent. / *blue*
327		PÉCS Zsolnay 2nd half of 19th cent. / *printed*
328		PÉCS Zsolnay 2nd half of 19th cent. / *printed*
329		VINOVO G. V. Brodel, cross of the Savoy dynasty 1776—1778 / *black*
330		VINOVO G. V. Brodel, Cross of the Savoy dynasty 1776—1778 / *blue*
331		VINOVO G. V. Brodel 1776—1778 / *blue*
332		VINOVO Dr V. A. Gioanetti after 1780 until 1815 / *blue*

333	**VINOVO** Porcelain factory, with the mark of the painter Carasso before 1820 / *blue*
334	**FULDA** city arms 1765—1775 / *blue*
335	**BRISTOL** R. Champion 1773—1781 / *blue*
336	**BRISTOL** R. Champion 1773—1781 / *blue*
337	**PLYMOUTH** W. Cookworthy after 1768—1770 / *blue or incised*
338	**BOURG LA REINE** J. Jullien & S. Jacques after 1773—1804 / *blue*
339	**SITZENDORF** Voigt Bros after 1850 / *blue*
340	**BERLIN** Royal Porcelain Factory from 1870 / *printed*
341	**COPENHAGEN** F. H. Müller after 1773 / *impressed*

342		PLAUE C. G. Schierholz & Sohn after 1817 / *blue*
343 **344**		PLAUE C. G. Schierholz & Sohn after 1817 / *blue*
345		SITZENDORF Voigt Bros after 1850 / *blue*
346		WORCESTER Mark of a painter from the Wall period 1751—1783 / *blue*
347		MARIEBERG H. Sten 1769—1788 / *blue*
348		BOW W. Duesbury 1760—1776 / *blue*
349 **350**		KORZEC Czartoryski-Mezer 1790—1797 / *gold*
351		CHELSEA Triangle period 1745—1749 / *incised*
352		CHELSEA Triangle period 1745—1749 / *printed*
353		WORCESTER Wall period 1751—1783 / *blue*
354 **355** **356**		WORCESTER Wall period 1751—1783 / *blue*
357		WORCESTER Wall period 1751—1783 / *blue*
358		WORCESTER Wall period 1751—1783 / *blue*

359		MOSCOW Kudinov 19th cent. / *blue*
360		ALCORA Count Aranda—P. Clooster- mans after 1786 / *brown, black*
361		ALCORA Count Aranda—P. Clooster- mans after 1786 / *gold*
362		ALCORA Count Aranda—P. Clooster- mans after 1786 / *incised*
363		BOW 3rd period, W. Duesbury 1760—1776 / *blue*
364		LONGTON HALL W. Littler 1750—1760 / *blue*
365		PARIS, RUE THIROUX A. M. Lebœuf 1776—1790 / *blue, red*
366		AICH (Doubí) J. Möhling 1849—1860 / *impressed*
367		TURN (Trnovany) Riessner & Kessel after 1892 / *printed*
368		ANSBACH Markgräfliche Porzellan- manufaktur after 1758 / *blue*
369		ANSBACH Markgräfliche Porzellan- manufaktur after 1758 / *blue*

370 371 372	ANSBACH Markgräfliche Porzellan- manufaktur after 1758 / *blue*
373	ANSBACH Markgräfliche Porzellan- manufaktur after 1758 / *blue*
374	SITZERODE G. H. Macheleid middle of 18th cent. / *blue*
375	ANSBACH Markgräfliche Porzellan- manufaktur *c.* 1765 / *blue*
376	ANSBACH Markgräfliche Porzellan- manufaktur *c.* 1765 / *blue*
377	ANSBACH Markgräfliche Porzellan- manufaktur *c.* 1765 / *blue*
378	ANSBACH mark of the palace porcelain 1757—1790 / *blue*
379	ANSBACH mark of the palace porcelain 1757—1790 / *blue*
380	ANSBACH mark of the palace porcelain 1757—1790 / *blue*

381 382 	**PARIS, RUE THIROUX** Manufacture de la Reine Marie Antoinette 1776—1790 / *blue, red*
383	**WEIDEN** A. Bauscher after 1881 / *blue*
384 	**ELGERSBURG** E. & F. C. Arnoldi second half of 19th cent. / *blue*
385 	**BAYREUTH** painter A. C. Wanderer 1727—1748 / *blue*
386	**ARZBERG** C. Schumann after 1881 / *printed*
387	**PARIS, GROS CAILLOU** Advenier & Lamare 1773—1784 / *blue*
388	**LONGTON** Adderley Watership end of 18th cent. / *printed*
389	**LONGTON** Adderley Watership beginning of 19th cent. *printed*

390		LONGTON Adderley Watership 19th cent. / *printed*
391		ILMENAU A. Fischer 1907 / *printed*
392		ILMENAU A. Fischer 1907 / *printed*
393		VIERZON H. Hachez & Co. 19th cent. / *printed*
394		AICH (Doubí) J. Möhling 1849 — 1860 / *impressed*
395		BUDAU (Budov) A. Lang 1860—1880 / *impressed*
396		LONGTON Royal Albert Bone China after 1844 / *printed*
397		LONGTON Royal Albert Bone China after 1844 / *printed*

398	Robert Allen 1760	LOWESTOFT R. Allen after 1780 / *blue*
399	allen Lowestoft	LOWESTOFT R. Allen after 1780 / *blue*
400		LOWESTOFT R. Allen after 1780 / *blue*
401		ALTENBURG 19th cent. / *printed*
402	ALTON BONE CHINA	LONGTON Alton China after 1950 / *printed*
403		ALT-ROHLAU (Stará Role) B. Hasslacher 1813—1824 / *impressed*
404		ALT-ROHLAU (Stará Role) A. Nowotny 1838—1884 / *impressed*
405		ALT-ROHLAU (Stará Role) M. Zdekauer 1884—1920 / *printed*

406	M Z Altrohlau CZECHOSLOVAKIA CMR	ALT-ROHLAU (Stará Role) M. Zdekauer after 1920 / *printed*
407	NOWOTNY IN ALTENROHLAU BEY KARLSBAD	ALT-ROHLAU (Stará Role) A. Nowotny 1838—1884 / *printed*
408	C. TIELSCH & Cᵒ ALTWASSER	WALDENBURG (Walbrzych) C. Tielsch 1845—1948 / *printed*
409	C.T. ALTWASSER	WALDENBURG (Walbrzych) C. Tielsch *c.* 1900 / *printed*
410	C.T. ALTWASSER	WALDENBURG (Walbrzych) C. Tielsch *c.* 1900 / *printed*
411	A M	AICH (Doubí) J. Möhling *c.* 1860 / *impressed*
412	A M	AICH (Doubí) J. Möhling before 1860 / *impressed*
413		KÖPPELSDORF-NORD A. Marseille after 1887 / *printed*
414		KÖPPELSDORF-NORD A. Marseille after 1887 / *blue*

415		SAINT AMAND LES EAUX Bettignies family 2nd half of 19th cent. / *blue*
416 **417**		AMBERG E. Kick after 1850—1910 / *blue*
418		TURN (Trnovany) Riessner & Kessel 20th cent. / *printed*
419		AMSTEL Däuber period 1784—1800 / *blue*
420		AMSTEL G. Dommer & Co. period 1801—1809 / *black, red, gold*
421		AMSTEL Däuber period 1784—1800 / *blue*
422		ALT-ROHLAU (Stará Role) A. Nowotny *c.* 1850 / *impressed*
423		ALT-ROHLAU (Stará Role) A. Nowotny *c.* 1870 / *impressed*
424		GUSTAVSBERG 1840 / *printed*
425		SAINT CLOUD / ROUEN? P. Chicaneau end of 17th cent. / *blue*

426 427		SAINT CLOUD / ROUEN? P. Chicaneau end of 17th cent. / *blue*
428		UNTERWEISSBACH A. Porzelius middle of 19th cent. / *printed*
429		MEISSEN Augustus Rex 1723—1736 / *blue*
430		MEISSEN Augustus Rex 1723—1736 / *blue*
431		MEISSEN Augustus Rex 1723—1736 / *blue*
432 433	AR AR	ARRAS J. F. Boussemart & Delemer 1770—1790 / *red*
434	AR ı	ARRAS J. F. Boussemart & Delemer 1770—1790 / *blue*
435	dele AR 2o	ARRAS Delemer 1772—1790 / *blue*
436	A.R P	ARRAS Delemer 1772—1790 / *blue*

437		MILAN A. Richard after 1850 / *blue*
438		COPENHAGEN A. Mollert 18th cent. / *impressed*
439		ELBOGEN (Loket) R. E. Haidinger imitations of Meissen 19th cent. / *blue*
440		WEIDEN Bauscher Bros after 1881 / *printed*
441		KÖNIGSZELT (Jaworzyna Śląska) A. Rosenthal & Co. *c.* 1900 / *printed*
442		ALT-ROHLAU (Stará Role) M. Zdekauer after 1880 / *printed*
443		HELSINKI "Arabia" after 1948 / *printed*
444		HELSINKI "Arabia" after 1948 / *printed*

445		HELSINKI "Arabia" after 1948 / *printed*
446	ARABIA	HELSINKI "Arabia" after 1948 / *printed*
447		DELFT Ary de Milde *c.* 1700 / *impressed*
448		ARZBERG a branch of the Kahl porcelain factory after 1890 / *printed*
449		ARZBERG C. M. Hutschenreuther after 1839 / *printed*
450		ARZBERG C. M. Hutschenreuther 2nd half of 19th cent. / *printed*
451 452		LONGTON Aynsley China 1st half of 19th cent. / *printed*
453		SAINT AMAND LES EAUX M. Bettignies 1st half of 19th cent. / *blue*

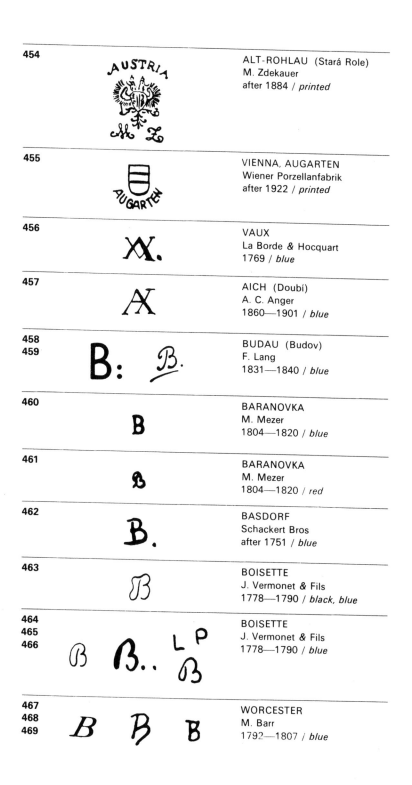

454

ALT-ROHLAU (Stará Role)
M. Zdekauer
after 1884 / *printed*

455

VIENNA, AUGARTEN
Wiener Porzellanfabrik
after 1922 / *printed*

456

VAUX
La Borde & Hocquart
1769 / *blue*

457

AICH (Doubí)
A. C. Anger
1860—1901 / *blue*

458
459

BUDAU (Budov)
F. Lang
1831—1840 / *blue*

460

BARANOVKA
M. Mezer
1804—1820 / *blue*

461

BARANOVKA
M. Mezer
1804—1820 / *red*

462

BASDORF
Schackert Bros
after 1751 / *blue*

463

BOISETTE
J. Vermonet & Fils
1778—1790 / *black, blue*

464
465
466

BOISETTE
J. Vermonet & Fils
1778—1790 / *blue*

467
468
469

WORCESTER
M. Barr
1792—1807 / *blue*

470		BOW W. Duesbury 1760—1776 / *blue, red*
471		BOW T. Frye 1755—1760 / *blue*
472		LASSAY L. L. F. Comte de Lauraguais-Brancas 1763—1768 / *incised*
473		BRUSSELS J. S. Vaume 1786—1790 / *blue, red*
474		BRUSSELS, SCHAERBEEK J. S. Vaume 1786—1790 / *blue, red*
475 476		BRISTOL W. Cookworthy 1773—1781 / *blue*
477		RUDOLSTADT E. Bohne from 1854 / *blue*
478		BARANOVKA M. Mezer after 1805 / *blue, gold*
479 480		BARANOVKA M. Mezer after 1805 / *red*
481		BARANOVKA M. Mezer after 1805—1825 / *red*
482		BARANOVKA M. Mezer after 1805—1825 / *blue*

483 484	*Baranowka* **B**	BARANOVKA M. Mezer after 1805—1825 / *black*
485	*Baranouka*	BARANOVKA M. Mezer after 1805—1825 / *black*
486	*Basdorf z.*	BASDORF Schackert Bros after 1751 / *blue*
487	Bavaria	PLANKENHAMMER after 1908 / *printed*
488	B C BAVARIA	WALDSASSEN Bayreuther & Co. after 1866 / *printed*
489	A C S BAVARIA	ARZBERG C. Schumann after 1881 / *printed*
490	GKC BAVARIA	WALDSASSEN Gareis, Kühnl & Co. after 1899 / *printed*
491	BAVARIA G·K·Co	WALDSASSEN Gareis, Kühnl & Co. after 1899 / *printed*
492	G. M. O BAVARIA	WALDSASSEN Gareis, Kühnl & Co. after 1899 / *printed*

493	HW ML BAVARIA	MARKTLEUTHEN H. Winterling after 1903 / *printed*
494	Gebr. BAVARIA	ERKERSREUTH Hoffmann Bros 20th cent. / *printed*
495	BAVARIA	SCHWARZENBACH J. Kronester & Co. after 1904 / *printed*
496	Bavaria	MITTERTEICH Porzellanfabrik A. G. after 1917 / *printed*
497	PMR BAVARIA Jaeger&Co	MARKTREDWITZ Jaeger & Co. after 1872 / *printed*
498	PYS BAVARIA	SELB P. Müller 1890—1912 / *printed*
499	BAVARIA	WUNSIEDEL Retsch & Co. after 1885 / *printed*
500	Bavaria	RÖSLAU Winterling Bros after 1906 / *printed*

501		HOF MOSCHENDORF O. Reinecke after 1878 / *printed*
502		SCHWARZENBACH O. Schaller & Co. after 1881 / *printed*
503		SCHWARZENBACH O. Schaller & Co. after 1917 / *printed*
504		MARKTLEUTHEN H. Winterling after 1903 / *printed*
505		REHAU Zeh, Scherzer & Co. after 1880 / *printed*
506		REHAU Zeh, Scherzer & Co. after 1880 / *printed*
507		REHAU Zeh, Scherzer & Co. after 1880 / *printed*
508		VALOGNES—BAYEUX M. F. Gosse after 1849 / *gold*
509		VALOGNES—BAYEUX W. Langlois before 1849 / *red*

510		VALOGNES—BAYEUX M. F. Gosse after 1849 / *red*
511		SOPHIENTHAL Thomas & Co. after 1948 / *printed*
512		SOPHIENTHAL Thomas & Co. 1928—1934 / *printed*
513		BAYREUTH S. P. Meyer, "Walkure" after 1900 / *printed*
514		WALDSASSEN Bayreuther & Co. after 1866 / *printed*
515	Bayswater	BAYSWATER English paint-room of Chinese and European porcelain 18th —19th cent. / *printed*
516		EICHWALD (Dubi) Bloch & Co. after 1871 / *blue*
517	BB	EICHWALD (Dubi) Bloch & Co. after 1871 / *blue*

518	B. D. J	SAINT AMAND LES EAUX J. B. Fauquez 1771—1778 / *blue*
519	FINE BONE *Bell* CHINA ENGLAND	LONGTON Shore & Coggins Ltd 19th cent. / *printed*
520	FINE BONE *Bell China* MADE IN ENGLAND	LONGTON Shore & Coggins Ltd 19th cent. / *printed*
521	BELLEEK	BELLEEK D. Birnay after 1863 / *printed*
522	BEM	MAGDEBURG-BUCKAU Buckauer Porzellanmanufaktur after 1832 / *blue*
523	BFB	WORCESTER Barr, Flight & Barr 1807—1813 / *impressed*
524	B.F.B.	WORCESTER Barr, Flight & Barr 1807—1813 / *blue*
525	B & G	COPENHAGEN Bing & Grøndahl 1854—1864 / *blue*
526	B·G DENMARK DANISH CHINA WORKS B & G	COPENHAGEN Bing & Grøndahl after 1854—1864 / *blue*

527	B & G	COPENHAGEN Bing & Grøndahl after 1854—1864 / *blue*
528		MAYERHÖFEN Benedikt Bros 1931—1945 / *printed*
529		LILLE F. & B. Dorez 1720—1730 / *blue*
530	BK	GIESSHÜBEL (Kysibl) B. Knaute 1828—1840 / *blue*
531	BLP.	REICHENSTEIN M. Blanka after 1831 / *blue*
532	B la R	BOURG LA REINE J. Jullien & S. Jacques after 1773—1804 / *impressed*
533	BLOOR DERBY	DERBY R. Bloor 1811—1849 / *printed*
534		DERBY R. Bloor 1811—1849 / *printed*
535		LE NOVE Fabbrica Antonibon 1762—1763 / *various colours,* *gold*

536

NIDERVILLER
J. L. de Beyerlé
1765—1770 / *red*

537

NIDERVILLER
J. L. de Beyerlé
1765—1770 / *blue*

538

NEU-ROHLAU (Nová Role)
"Bohemia"
1921 / *printed*

539

NEU-ROHLAU (Nová Role)
"Bohemia"
1921 / *printed*

540

VIENNA
G. Mladenof & Co.
after 1929 / *printed*

541

FENTON
A. Bowker
19th cent. / *printed*

542

BORDEAUX
D. Johnston
1836—1845 / *violet*

543

LONGTON
Cartwright & Edwards Ltd.
after 1858 / *printed*

544	**B Potter 42**	PARIS, RUE DE CRUSSOL C. Potter 1792—1800 / *blue*
545		BORDEAUX Verneuilh & Alluaud 1781—1790 / *impressed*
546	**B . R .**	BOURG LA REINE J. Jullien & S. Jacques after 1773—1804 / *impressed*
547	B R N	BOURG LA REINE J. Jullien & S. Jacques after 1773—1804 / *impressed*
548	**BRAMELD**	SWINTON Rockingham Factory 19th cent. / *printed*
549
Branksome China England	BOURNEMOUTH Branksome Ceramics after 1945 / *printed*
550	*Bristol*	BRISTOL R. Champion 1773—1781 / *red*
551	**Bristol** founded X in 1652 **England** B	BRISTOL Putney & Co. after 1852 / *printed*

552		BRUSSELS, ETTERBEEK L. Demeuldre-Coché 1920—1930 / *printed*
553		BRUSSELS, ETTERBEEK L. Demeuldre-Coché 1920—1941 / *printed*
554		BRUSSELS, ETTERBEEK L. Demeuldre-Coché 1920—1941 / *printed*
555		BRUSSELS, ETTERBEEK Etablissements Demeuldre 20th cent. / *printed*
556	L.C Brux	BRUSSELS L. Cretté 1791—1803 / *red*
557		BUDAPEST E. Fischer after 1868 / *printed*

558		SHELTON Brow, Westerheat & Co. after 1858 / *printed*
559	C	CAUGHLEY T. Turner after 1772—1783 / *blue*
560	C	CHODAU (Chodov) Hüttner & Co. 1835—1840 / *blue, gold*
561	C	CHODAU (Chodov) Haas & Czjizek after 1905 / *blue*
562	/C\	CHODZIEŻ Fabryka porcelany after 1882 / *blue*
563	/Ć\	ĆMIELÓW X. Drucko-Lubecki after 1842 / *blue*
564	(A)	UHLSTÄDT R. Albert after 1873 / *blue*
565	FRANCE ... DÉPOSÉ	LIMOGES C. Ahrenfeld after 1894 / *printed*
566	A	LIMOGES C. Ahrenfeld end of 19th cent. / *printed*
567	**CAEN**	CAEN d'Aigmont-Desmares 1793—1806 / *red*
568	**caen**	CAEN d'Aigmont-Desmares 1793—1806 / *red*

569	CARLSBAD	FISCHERN (Rybáře) C. Knoll 1848—1868 / *impressed*
570		DELFT J. Caluve before 1730 / *impressed*
571	 ESTᵈ. 1774 **CAULDON CHINA** **ENGLAND**	SHELTON Cauldon China 20th cent. / *printed*
572	CBD	COALPORT (COALBROOKDALE) after 1780 / *blue*
573		COALPORT (COALBROOKDALE) after 1780 / *blue*
574		COALPORT (COALBROOKDALE) after 1780 / *blue*
575		COALPORT (COALBROOKDALE) after 1780 / *blue, gold*
576	 C B DALE	COALPORT (COALBROOKDALE) after 1780 / *blue, gold*
577		NIDERVILLER A. P. de Custine 1770—1793 / *black*
578		LUDWIGSBURG Carl Eugen of Württemberg 1759—1793 / *blue*

579		LUDWIGSBURG Carl Eugen of Württemberg 1759—1793 / *blue*
580		NIDERVILLER A. P. de Custine 1770—1793 / *blue*
581		NIDERVILLER A. P. de Custine 1770—1793 / *blue*
582		LUDWIGSBURG Carl Eugen of Württemberg 1759—1793 / *blue*
583		LUDWIGSBURG Carl Eugen of Württemberg 1759—1806 / *blue*
584		LUDWIGSBURG Carl Eugen of Württemberg 1759—1806 / *blue*
585		ROME F. Cuccumos 1761—1781 / *blue*
586		SCHORNDORF C. M. Bauer & Pfeiffer after 1904—1939 / *printed*
587		COALPORT (COALBROOKDALE) after 1780 / *blue*
588		LIMOGES Grellet Frères after 1771—1796 / *blue, impressed, red, gold*

589	*c d*	LIMOGES Grellet Frères after 1771—1796 / *blue,* *impressed, red, gold*
590	*C·D*	LIMOGES Grellet Frères after 1771—1796 / *blue,* *impressed, red, gold*
591	C·D	LIMOGES Grellet Frères 1771—1796 / *blue*
592	C&E / C	SORAU (Žary) C. & E. Carstens after 1918 / *printed*
593	C · G W	WÜRZBURG C. Geyger 1775—1780 / *impressed*
594	CF	ZWICKAU C. Fischer after 1850 / *blue*
595	CF	PIRKENHAMMER (Březová) C. Fischer 1846—1857 / *impressed*
596	*CF....*	MILAN San Cristoforo 1830—1833 / *blue*
597	C *Flight*	WORCESTER J. & J. Flight 1783—1791 / *red, blue*
598	CH	PARIS, BARRIÈRE DE REUILLY H. F. Chanou 1779—1785 / *red, gold*
599	CHAMBERLAINS WORCESTER.	WORCESTER R. Chamberlain after 1840 / *blue*
600	*Chamberlain's* *Worcester* *& 63, Piccadilly,* *London*	WORCESTER Chamberlains after 1840 / *printed*

601		WORCESTER R. Chamberlain c. 1850 / *blue*
602		WORCESTER Chamberlains 1852—1862 / *printed*
603	CHAMBERLAIN & CO. WORCESTER 155 NEW BOND STREET & NO. 1 COVENTRY ST LONDON	WORCESTER Chamberlains 1840—1845 / *printed*
604	*Chamberlain's* *Worcester* *& 155* *New Bond Street* *London*	WORCESTER Chamberlains 1840—1845 / *printed*
605		WORCESTER Chamberlains 1840—1845 / *printed*
606	**CHAMBERLAINS**	WORCESTER Chamberlains from 1840 / *printed*
607		STOKE-ON-TRENT Mintons Ltd from 1911 / *printed*
608		CHANTILLY Prince de Condé 1760—1800 / *blue*

609	*chatillon*	CHATILLON Porcelain factory after 1775 / *blue*
610	D⚓V *Chatillon*	CHATILLON Porcelain factory after 1775 / *blue*
611	△ *Chelsea 1745*	CHELSEA N. Sprimont & C. Gouyn 1745—1749 / *incised*
612	Chodau	CHODAU (Chodov) Haas & Czjizek after 1920 / *impressed*
613	CHODAU H ♣ C CZJIZEK	CHODAU (Chodov) Haas & Czjizek after 1920 / *printed*
614	CHODAU H ♣ C CZECHOSLOVAKIA	CHODAU (Chodov) Haas & Czjizek after 1920 / *printed*
615	Porcelit ✕ Chodziez P	CHODZIEŻ Fabryka porcelany after 1882 / *printed*
616	C CHODZIEŻ	CHODZIEŻ Fabryka porcelany after 1882 / *printed*
617	⚜	MANTUA, CANETTO SULL'OGLIO Ceramica Furga after 1872 / *blue*
618	CL	NIDERVILLER C. Lanfrey 1792—1827 / *blue*
619	CL	NIDERVILLER C. Lanfrey 1792—1827 / *blue*

620		HOHENBERG C. M. Hutschenreuther 1865 / *printed*
621		ĆMIELÓW Fabryka porcelany 1842—1863 / *blue*
622		NIDERVILLER A. P. de Custine 1770—1802 / *blue*
623		NIDERVILLER A. P. de Custine 1770—1802 / *blue*
624		COALPORT Coalport China 2nd half of 19th cent. / *blue*
625		COALPORT Coalport China 1st half of 20th cent. / *printed*
626		COALPORT Coalport China 20th cent. / *printed*
627		COALPORT Coalport China 20th cent. / *printed*
628		HANLEY Booths & Colclough Ltd. 20th cent. / *printed*

629		HANLEY Booths & Colclough Ltd. 20th cent. / *printed*
630		HANLEY Booths & Colclough Ltd. 20th cent. / *printed*
631		LONGTON Collingwood Bros Ltd. 20th cent. / *printed*
632		STOKE-ON-TRENT W. T. Copeland after 1829—20th cent. / *blue*
633		STOKE-ON-TRENT W. T. Copeland after 1829—20th cent. / *blue*
634	**Copeland late Spode**	STOKE-ON-TRENT W. T. Copeland 1847—1867 / *blue*
635		STOKE-ON-TRENT W. T. Copeland after 1870 / *blue*
636	SPODE COPELANDS CHINA ENGLAND	STOKE-ON-TRENT W. T. Copeland 1847—1867 / *blue*
637	Copeland Stone China	STOKE-ON-TRENT W. T. Copeland 1847—1867 / *blue*
638		STOKE-ON-TRENT W. T. Copeland 20th cent. / *printed*

639		STOKE-ON-TRENT W. T. Copeland 20th cent. / *printed*
640		STOKE-ON-TRENT W. T. Copeland & Garrett 1833—1846 / *printed*
641		STOKE-ON-TRENT W. T. Copeland & Garrett 1833—1846 / *printed*
642		STOKE-ON-TRENT W. T. Copeland & Garrett 1833—1846 / *printed*
643		STOKE-ON-TRENT W. T. Copeland & Garrett 1833—1846 / *printed*
644		STOKE-ON-TRENT W. T. Copeland & Garrett 1833—1846 / *printed*
645		STOKE-ON-TRENT W. T. Copeland & Garrett 1833—1846 / *printed*
646		STOKE-ON-TRENT W. T. Copeland & Garrett 1833—1846 / *printed*

647		STOKE-ON-TRENT W. T. Copeland & Garrett 1833—1846 / *printed*
648	**COPELAND** **& GARRETT**	STOKE-ON-TRENT W. T. Copeland & Garrett 1833—1846 / *printed*
649		COBURG A. Riemann after 1860/*printed*
650		CREIDLITZ Porzellanfabrik A. G. after 1907 / *printed*
651	*crepy*	CRÉPY EN VALOIS L. F. Gaignepain & P. Bourgeois 1762—1767 / *incised*
652	D, C, P,	CRÉPY EN VALOIS L. F. Gaignepain & P. Bourgeois 1762—1767 / *incised*
653	*c . p .*	CRÉPY EN VALOIS L. F. Gaignepain & P. Bourgeois 1762—1767 / *incised*
654 655	**CP CP**	PARIS, RUE FAUBOURG SAINT DENIS Comte d'Artois 1779—1793 / *blue, red*
656	**CPM**	ĆMIELÓW Fabryka porcelany *c.* 1850 / *blue*
657		COPENHAGEN Royal Porcelain Factory 1889 / *green*

658		COPENHAGEN Dahl-Jensens Porcelaensfabrik after 1925 / *green*
659		COPENHAGEN Royal Porcelain Factory 1897 / *green*
660		COPENHAGEN Royal Porcelain Factory 1923 / *green*
661		COPENHAGEN Bing & Grøndahl after 1854 / *blue*
662		COPENHAGEN Bing & Grøndahl 1905 / *red, various colours*
663		COPENHAGEN Bing & Grøndahl 1914 / *red, various colours*
664		SCHWARZA-SAALBAHN E. & A. Müller after 1890 / *blue*

665	*L. C.* *Ebenſtein*	BRUSSELS L. Cretté 1791—1803 / *blue*
666	*L. cretté* *Brux*	BRUSSELS L. Cretté 1791—1803 / *red, brown*
667	*L. c*	BRUSSELS L. Cretté 1791—1803 / *red, brown*
668	*L . cretté.* *Bruxelles rue* *D'Aremberg* *1791*	BRUSSELS L. Cretté 1791—1803 / *red, brown*
669		COALPORT Caughley, Swansea, Nantgarw after 1861 / *blue*
670	C.T.	WALDENBURG (Walbrzych) C. Tielsch after 1945 / *blue*
671	C.T.	POTSCHAPPEL C. Thieme after 1872 / *blue*
672	C.T.	WALDENBURG (Walbrzych) C. Tielsch after 1845 / *blue*
673	C. T.	POTSCHAPPEL C. Thieme 20th cent. / *printed*

674		WALDENBURG (Walbrzych) C. Tielsch after 1845 / *blue*
675		KLOSTER VEILSDORF W. E. von Hildburghausen before 1765 / *blue*
676		KLOSTER VEILSDORF W. E. von Hildburghausen 1760—1797 / *blue*
677		KLOSTER VEILSDORF W. E. von Hildburghausen 1760—1797 / *blue*
678		SCHLACKENWERTH (Ostrov) Pfeiffer & Löwenstein after 1918 / *printed*
679		LUNÉVILLE P. L. Cyfflé 1766—1780 / *blue*
680		ALT-ROHLAU (Stará Role) M. Zdekauer after 1918 / *printed*
681 682		DERBY W. Duesbury & J. Heath 1770—1784 / *gold*
683		DERBY W. Duesbury & J. Heath after 1750 / *incised*
684		DERBY W. Duesbury & J. Heath 1770—1784 / *red, gold*
685		DERBY W. Duesbury & J. Heath 1770—1784 / *gold*

686		DERBY W. Duesbury & J. Heath 1784—1811 / *blue, red, gold*
687		DERBY W. Duesbury 1784—1810 / *incised*
688		DERBY W. Duesbury 1784—1810 / *blue, red*
689		DERBY R. Bloor 1811—1848 / *blue, red*
690		DERBY W. Duesbury 1784—1810 / *blue, red*
691		DERBY R. Bloor 1811—1848 / *printed, red*
692		DERBY Stevenson & Handcock 1850—1870 / *red*
693		DRESDEN 19th cent. / *blue*
694		DALLWITZ (Dalovice) V. W. Lorenz 1831—1850 / *impressed*

695		DUISDORF "Rhenania" after 1904 / *printed*
696		BRUSSELS, ETTERBEEK H. Demeuldre 20th cent. / *printed*
697		VINOVO G. Balbo *c.* 1800 / *red, green*
698		DALLWITZ (Dalovice) V. W. Lorenz 1832—1850 / *impressed*
699		STOKE-ON-TRENT Minton & Boyle 1836—1841 / *printed*
700		COALPORT (COALBROOKDALE) end of 18th cent. / *blue*
701	DALWITZ	DALLWITZ (Dalovice) V. W. Lorenz 1832—1850 / *impressed*
702	W.W.L. DALWITZ	DALLWITZ (Dalovice) V. W. Lorenz 1832—1850 / *impressed*
703		DAMM Steingut- und Porzellanfabrik 1827—1884 / *impressed*

704		COPENHAGEN Royal Porcelain Factory 1894 / *green, blue*
705		PARIS, RUE DE CHARONNE Darte Frères *c.* 1800 / *red*
706		PARIS, RUE DE CHARONNE Darte Frères *c.* 1800 / *red*
707		LONGPORT Davenport 1793—1882 / *blue, printed*
708		LONGPORT Davenport 1793—1882 / *blue, printed*
709		WORCESTER Flight & Barr 1792—1807 / *incised*
710		COALPORT (COALBROOKDALE) *c.* 1850 / *blue*
711 712		PARIS, CLIGNANCOURT P. Deruelle 1775—1793 / *red*
713		CRÉPY EN VALOIS L. Gaignepain & L. Bourgeois 1762—1767 / *blue*
714		CRÉPY EN VALOIS L. Gaignepain & L. Bourgeois 1762—1767 / *blue*

715  ARRAS
Delemer
1772—1790 / *blue*

716 COPENHAGEN
Royal Porcelain Factory
1890 / *red, green*

717 LONGTON
Denton China Company
20th cent. / *printed*

718 DERBY
A. Planché
1750 / *incised*

719 DERBY
W. Duesbury
after 1770—1784 / *red*

720 DERBY
R. Bloor
1850—1870 / *red*

721  DERBY
R. Bloor
1811—1849 / *blue, red*

722 DERBY
R. Bloor
1811—1849 / *red*

723 DERBY
Locker & Co.
1849—1870 / *red*

724		DERBY Stevenson, Sharp & Co. 1859 / *red*
725	DUESBURY DERBY	DERBY W. Duesbury 1784—1810 / *red*
726		DERBY W. Duesbury 1784—1810 / *red*
727	D G	VINOVO Dr. V. A. Gioanetti after 1780 / *blue*
728		CHODAU (Chodov) J. Hüttner & Co. 1835—1840 / *impressed*
729	 DIAMANT J&C	MARKTREDWITZ Jaeger & Co. after 1872 / *printed*
730		LONGTON A. T. Finney & Sons Ltd 20th cent. / *printed*
731	*Dihl.*	PARIS, RUE DE BONDY J. Dihl 1817—1829 / *blue, red*

732		**DERBY** W. Duesbury & M. Kean 1795—1796 / *blue, red*
733		**DERBY** W. Duesbury & M. Kean 1795—1796 / *red, blue*
734 735 736		**GRÄFENRODA** Dornheim, Koch & Fischer after 1860 / *blue*
737	DILLWYN &C. SWANSEA.	**SWANSEA** L. W. Dillwyn 1814—1850 / *printed*
738		**TIEFENFURTH** (Parowa) P. Donath after 1883 / *printed*
739	*Donovan's Irish Manufactur*	**DUBLIN** Donovan & Son beginning of 19th cent. / *red*
740	*Donovan's Irish Manufacture*	**DUBLIN** Donovan & Son beginning of 19th cent. / *red, violet*
741	**Donovan Dublin**	**DUBLIN** Donovan & Son beginning of 19th cent. / *red*
742	DONOVAN 481	**DUBLIN** Donovan & Son beginning of 19th cent. / *blue*
743		**BURSLEM** Doulton & Co. after 1815 / *printed*

744

BURSLEM
Doulton & Co.
after 1815 / *printed*

745

BURSLEM
Doulton & Co.
after 1815 / *printed*

746

BURSLEM
Doulton & Co.
after 1815 / *printed*

747

DRESDEN
19th cent. / *blue*

748

KRONACH
P. Rosenthal & Co.
end of 19th cent. / *blue*

749

LONGTON
Dresden Floral Porcelain Co.
from 1845 / *printed*

750

DRESDEN
Dresdner Porzellanmanufaktur
20th cent. / *printed*

751		POTSCHAPPEL C. Thieme after 1872 / *printed*
752		DRESDEN Dresdner Porzellanmanufaktur 20th cent. / *printed*
753		DERBY W. Duesbury 1803 / *red*
754		LONGTON A. T. Finney & Sons Ltd 20th cent. / *printed*
755		GATESHEAD Durham China Company 20th cent. / *printed*
756		DUISDORF "Rhenania" after 1904 / *printed*
757	.D.V.	MENNECY Duc de Villeroy 1740—1773 / *incised*
758	.D.V.	MENNECY Duc de Villeroy 1734—1740 / *blue and other colours*

759	**D . V'**	MENNECY Duc de Villeroy 1734—1740 / *blue, red, black, brown*
760	**D.V**	MENNECY Duc de Villeroy 1734—1740 / *red, blue, black, brown*
761	**E**	EICHWALD (Dubí) Bloch & Co. after 1871 / *blue*
762	**E** Made in Czechoslovakia	EICHWALD (Dubí) Bloch & Co. after 1920 / *blue*
763	ORIGINAL **E·**	EICHWALD (Dubí) Bloch & Co. *c.* 1900 / *blue*
764	**Ɛ·**	EISENBERG F. A. Reinecke after 1796 / *blue*
765	**Ɛ** *Pelleve 1770*	ETIOLLES D. Pellevé *c.* 1770 / *incised*
766	**ÉB**	PARIS, RUE DE CRUSSOL E. Blancheron 1792—1807 / *blue*
767	B ⤬ S E	EISENBERG Bremer & Schmidt after 1895 / *printed*
768	DUPOMA E	DUX (Duchcov) E. Eichler after 1860 / *printed*

769		DUX (Duchcov) E. Eichler *c.* 1900 / *printed*
770		POSCHETZAU (Božičany) Maier & Co. after 1890 / *printed*
771		EICHWALD (Dubí) Bloch & Co. after 1918 / *printed*
772		EICHWALD (Dubí) Bloch & Co. after 1871 / *printed*
773		EISENBERG W. Jäger after 1867 / *printed*
774		ELGERSBURG E. & F. C. Arnoldi after 1808 / *printed*
775		MERKELSGRÜN (Merklín) "Elsa" Porzellan 1900 until 1918 / *printed*
776		MIDDLETON *c.* 1870 / *printed*

777		LONGTON Cartwright & Edwards Ltd after 1858 / *printed*
778 779		VOLKSTEDT-RUDOLSTADT K. Ens after 1898 / *printed*
780		AICH (Doubi) "Epiag" after 1918 / *printed*
781		ALT-ROHLAU (Stará Role) "Epiag" after 1918 / *printed*
782		TILLOWITZ (Tulowice) Reinholdt & Schlegelmilch after 1869 / *printed*
783		ERBENDORF C. Seltmann after 1940 / *printed*
784		ERBENDORF C. Seltmann after 1940 / *printed*
785 786		WINDISCH-ESCHENBACH O. Schaller & Co. and successors after 1913 / *printed*
787		STADTLENGSFELD Porzellanfabrik A. G. c. 1900 / *printed*

788	*Eterbeek*	BRUSSELS, ETTERBEEK C. Kuhne 1787—1803 / *incised*
789	*Etiolle* *x bre 1770* *Pelleve*	ETIOLLES D. Pellevé *c.* 1770 / *incised*
790 791	*F* *J*	FÜRSTENBERG Charles I of Brunswick 1753—1770 / *blue*
792 793	*F* *F*	FÜRSTENBERG Charles I of Brunswick 1770—1800 / *blue*
794		FÜRSTENBERG Herzogliche Porzellan- manufaktur 20th cent. / *blue*
795		FÜRSTENBERG Herzogliche Porzellan- manufaktur 1800—1860 / *blue*
796	*I*	WORCESTER Dr Wall 1751—1783 / *blue*
797	⅂ ••	BOW T. Frye 1755—1760 / *blue*
798		PARIS, RUE DE LA PAIX J. Feuillet after 1820 / *green*
799		VOLKSTEDT-RUDOLSTADT E. Bohne 19th cent. / *blue*
800	Ⓕ	FRAUREUTH Römer & Födisch 2nd half of 19th cent. / *blue*

801		FRAUREUTH Römer & Födisch 2nd half of 19th cent. / *blue*
802		COPENHAGEN Royal Porcelain Factory (monogram of Frederick V) 1760—1766 / *blue*
803		MEISSEN Frederick Augustus III after 1733 / *blue*
804		SELB P. Müller, "Favorit" 1890—1912 / *printed*
805		GRÜNSTADT F. Bartholdi 19th cent. / *blue*
806		WORCESTER Flight, Barr & Barr 1813—1840 / *printed, impressed*
807		WORCESTER Flight, Barr & Barr 1813—1840 / *impressed*
808		STADTLENGSFELD Porzellanfabrik A. G. after 1889 / *printed*
809		FULDA Heinrich VIII von Bibra 1770—1788 / *blue*
810		FULDA Adalbert III von Harstall 1788—1789 / *blue*

811	**F.F.**	TREVISO G. & A. Fontebasso c. 1800 / *blue*
812		SAINT AMAND LES EAUX J. B. Fauquez 1771—1778 / *blue*
813	**F.F.** **D.**	DALLWITZ (Dalovice) F. Fischer 1850—1855 / *impressed*
814		VOLKSTEDT-RUDOLSTADT F. Greiner 20th cent. / *printed*
815	F K O ⚒ Z	OBERHOHNDORF F. Kaestner 1883—20th cent. / *printed*
816		VALENCIENNES J. B. Fauquez & Lamoninary 1785—1795 / *blue*
817	FL	BUDAU (Budov) F. Lang 1840—1860 / *impressed*
818	*Flight*	WORCESTER J. & J. Flight 1783—1792 / *blue*
819 820	*Flight* *Flight*	WORCESTER J. & J. Flight 1783—1792 / *red, blue*
821	**FLIGHTS**	WORCESTER J. & J. Flight 1783—1792 / *impressed*
822	*Flight & Barr*	WORCESTER J. & J. Flight 1783—1792 / *blue*

823	*Flight*	WORCESTER Flight & Barr 1792—1807 / *impressed,* *printed*
824	*Flight Barr & Barr*	WORCESTER Flight, Barr & Barr 1813—1840 / *impressed,* *printed*
825		WILHELMSBURG Aktiengesellschaft after 1882 / *printed*
826		STOKE-ON-TRENT Mintons & Hollins 1846—1868 / *printed*
827	F & M	PIRKENHAMMER (Březová) Fischer & Mieg 1810—1846 / *impressed*
828	Fontaine F. 1770	LIMOGES Grellet Frères & Massié 1770—1796 / *blue*
829		FOËCY Pillivuyt family after 1800 / *blue*
830		FOËCY L. Lourioux 2nd half of 19th cent. / *printed*
831	FOLEY ENGLISH BONE CHINA PAINTED BY HAND 	FENTON E. Brain & Co. after 1880 / *printed*

832	ESTABLISHED 18 R & S 50 L FOLEY CHINA	FENTON Robinson & Son after 1850 / printed
833		FRAUREUTH Porzellanfabrik after 1866 / printed
834	F P Nd.Salzbrunn	NIEDER-SALZBRUNN (Szczawienko) F. Prause from 1899 / blue
835 836	F.P.C. F.P.C.	ĆMIELÓW K. Cybulski 1870—1884 / black, impressed
837	FPM	FREIWALDAU (Gozdnica) H. Schmidt after 1842 / blue
838		NAPLES Ferdinand IV Rex 1772 / blue
839	F&R	PIRKENHAMMER (Březová) Fischer & Reichenbach 1811—1845 / impressed
840	L L FRANCE	FOËCY L. Lourioux 2nd half of 19th cent. / printed
841	FRAUREUTH	FRAUREUTH Porzellanfabrik after 1866 / printed
842	FU	DALLWITZ (Dalovice) F. Urfus 1855—1875 / impressed
843	FURGA	MANTUA, CANETTO SULL'OGLIO Ceramica Furga after 1872 / printed

844		BOW E. Heylyn & T. Frye 1748—1755 / *blue*
845 **846**		VERBILKI F. Gardner after 1767—1800 / *blue*
847		GERA J. G. Ehwaldt, J. Gottbrecht and successors 1779—1820 / *blue*
848 **849**		GOTHA E. Henneberg 1805—1834 / *blue, various colours*
850 **851**		BERLIN J. E. Gotzkowsky 1761—1763 / *blue, gold*
852		GEHREN J. Günthersfeld & Co. after 1884 / *printed*
853		DOCCIA Ginori 1884—1888 / *impressed*
854		LE NOVE G. B. Antonibon 1762—1802 / *blue, impressed*
855		PARIS, RUE DE BONDY Manufacture du duc d'Angoulême 1781—1793 / *red, gold, blue*

856		PARIS, RUE DE BONDY Manufacture du duc d'Angoulême 1781—1793 / *red, gold*
857		ILMENAU Galluba & Hofmann after 1888 / *printed*
858		ILMENAU Galluba & Hofmann after 1888 / *printed*
859	G B	GRÜNSTADT F. Bartholdi after 1801 / *blue*
860		GROSSBREITENBACH H. Bühl & Söhne after 1780 / *blue*
861		UPPSALA "Gefle" Porslin after 1910 / *printed*
862		UPPSALA "Gefle" Porslin after 1910 / *printed*
863		ALT-ROHLAU (Stará Role) Porzellanfabrik Viktoria A. G. after 1883 / *printed*
864	P Manufacture de J. Mulhauser Geneve	GENEVA J. P. Mühlhauser 1805—1818 / *blue*

865	**P.M** *Genève*	GENEVA J. P. Mühlhauser 1805—1818 / *blue*
866 **867**		GERONA "Cordoba" 19th cent. / *blue, red*
868		OBERKOTZAU Greiner & Herda after 1893 / *printed*
869		KATOWICE Giesche end of 19th cent. / *blue*
870 **871**		GIESSHÜBEL (Kysibl) F. Lehnert 1840—1847 / *impressed*
872		GIESSHÜBEL (Kysibl) W. von Neuberg 1846—1902 / *impressed*
873	**GI**	DOCCIA Ginori 1868—1903 / *blue*
874 **875**	**GIN GINORI**	DOCCIA Ginori 1868—1903 / *impressed*
876	**Ginori**	DOCCIA Ginori 1884—1901 / *impressed*
877		MILAN Richard —Ginori 1903 / *printed*

878		OESLAU W. Goebel after 1879 / *printed*
879		GOTHA August von Gotha c. 1805 / *blue*
880		GOTHA E. Henneberg middle of 19th cent. / *blue*
881		GOTHA Morgenroth & Co. after 1866 / *printed*
882		GOTHA E. Pfeffer after 1892 / *blue*
883		UNTERNHAUS Gerarer Porzellanfabrik after 1780 /·*blue*
884		GOTHA E. Pfeffer after 1892 / *blue*
885	GRAINGER & CO	WORCESTER Grainger & Co. after 1885 / *blue*
886	*Grainger Lee & Co* *Worcester*	WORCESTER Grainger, Lee & Co. after 1889 / *blue*
887		GRÄFENTHAL Weiss, Kühnert & Co. after 1891 / *printed*

888	Greiner 1768 ✗✗	VOLKSTEDT-RUDOLSTADT W. Greiner after 1799 / *impressed, blue*
889	Asiatic Treasure GUSTAFSBERG	GUSTAVSBERG Ceramic Factory 1845—1880 / *printed*
890	MINERVA GUSTAFSBERG	GUSTAVSBERG Ceramic Factory 1866 / *blue*
891	GUSTAVSBERG ⚓	GUSTAVSBERG Ceramic Factory 1910—1940 / *blue*
892	GUSTAVSBERG ⚓ STOCKHOLM	GUSTAVSBERG Ceramic Factory 1930 / *printed*
893 894	GUSTAVSBERG ⚓ LANDSKAP KÅGE GUSTAVSBERG ⚓ GULDSTJARNA KÅGE	GUSTAVSBERG Ceramic Factory 1924 / *printed*
895	GUSTAVSBERG ⚓ IVORY BONE CHINA SWEDEN KÅGE	GUSTAVSBERG Ceramic Factory 1928 / *printed*
896	SAFIR Gustafsberg J.J.F.	GUSTAVSBERG Ceramic Factory 1930 / *printed*
897 898		GUSTAVSBERG Ceramic Factory 1940 / *printed*

899		GUSTAVSBERG Ceramic Factory 1943 / *printed*
900		GEHREN P. Günthersfeld after 1884 / *printed*
901 902	M. H	STRASBOURG (HAGENAU) J. A. Hannong after 1768—1784 / *blue*
903 904		STRASBOURG P. A. Hannong (Hagenau factory) 1783—1784 / *blue*
905		PARIS, RUE DE FAUBOURG SAINT DENIS P. A. Hannong 1771—1776 / *blue*
906	H	LOWESTOFT R. Haward after 1761 / *blue*
907	H	MOSCOW D. Nasonov 1811—1813 / *blue*
908		LICHTE Heubach Bros after 1820 / *blue*
909		MANNHEIM Rheinische Porzellanfabrik 19th cent. / *impressed*
910 911		HÜTTENSTEINACH Schoenau Bros after 1865 / *blue*

912	*August Haas' in Schlaggenwald*	SCHLAGGENWALD (Slavkov) A. Haas 1847—1867 / *printed*
913	*August Haas in Schlaggenwald*	SCHLAGGENWALD (Slavkov) A. Haas 1847—1867 / *printed*
914	*August Haas in Schlaggenwald*	SCHLAGGENWALD (Slavkov) A. Haas 1847—1867 / *printed*
915	**Haas & Čžjžek in Schlaggenwald**	SCHLAGGENWALD (Slavkov) Haas & Czjizek after 1867 / *impressed*
916	HACKEFORS	HACKEFORS J. O. Nilson after 1929 / *printed*
917	*Hadley* WORCESTER ENGLAND	WORCESTER Hadley after 1905 / *printed*
918	Haidinger	ELBOGEN (Loket) Haidinger Bros 1833—1873 / *impressed*
919	Bone China Hammersley & Co MADE IN ENGLAND	LONGTON Hammersley & Co. 1860—1870 / *printed*
920	**Robt Havard 1761**	LOWESTOFT R. Haward after 1761 / *blue*

921		WALDERSHOF J. Haviland 1907—1924 / *printed*
922		KELSTERBACH Ludwig VIII of Hesse-Darm-stadt 1767—1768 / *impressed*
923		GROSSBREITENBACH H. Bühl & Söhne after 1780 / *blue, printed*
924		KASSEL Friedrich II of Hesse-Kassel 1766—1788 / *blue*
925		NEUSTADT Heber & Co. after 1900 / *printed*
926		LIMOGES Haviland & Co. after 1797 / *blue*
927		SELB Heinrich & Co. after 1896 / *printed*
928		KELSTERBACH Ludwig VIII of Hesse-Darmstadt 1767—1768 / *blue*
929		KELSTERBACH J. J. Lay 1789—1792 / *incised*
930		KELSTERBACH 1799—1802 / *blue*
931		HELSINKI "Arabia" after 1948 / *printed*

932

HELSINKI
"Arabia"
after 1948 / *printed*

933

HEREND
Porcelain Factory
1855—1898 / *blue*

934

HEREND
Porcelain Factory
1891—1897 / *blue*

935
936

HEREND
Porcelain Factory
1939 / *blue*

937

HEREND
Porcelain Factory
1940 / *blue*

938

HEREND
Porcelain Factory
1899—1939 / *blue*

939

HEREND
Porcelain Factory
1897—1938 / *blue*

940

HEREND
Porcelain Factory
1941 / *blue*

941

HEREND
Porcelain Factory
1855—1898 / *blue*

942		HEREND Porcelain Factory 1933—1938 / *blue*
943		LICHTE Heubach Bros after 1820 / *blue*
944 945		STRASBOURG J. A. Hannong 1768—1781 / *blue*
946		FENTON E. Hughes after 1883 / *printed*
947		BOULOGNE Haffringue beginning of 19th cent. / *blue*
948		STRASBOURG J. A. Hannong 1768—1784 / *blue*
949 950		HÜTTENSTEINACH Schoenau Bros after 1865 / *blue*
951		PIRKENHAMMER (Březová) Friedrich Höcke 1803—1810 / *blue, gold*
952		VINCENNES P. A. Hannong & La Borde 1769—1770 / *blue*
953 954		VINCENNES P. A. Hannong & La Borde 1769—1770 / *blue*

955		**LETTIN** H. Baensch beginning of 20th cent. *printed*
956		**COPENHAGEN** J. J. Holm *c.* 1780 / *impressed*
957		**LONGTON** Hudson & Middleton after 1870 / *printed*
958		**COPENHAGEN** J. J. Holm *c.* 1780 / *impressed*
959		**PROBSTZELLA** H. Hutschenreuther after 1886 / *printed*
960		**VIERZON** Hachez & Pépin *c.* 1879 / *blue*
961		**HOHENBERG** C. M. Hutschenreuther 1828—1845 / *impressed*
962		**HOHENBERG** C. M. Hutschenreuther and successors 1890 / *printed*
963		**HOHENBERG** Hutschenreuther 1914 / *printed*
964		**HOHENBERG** Hutschenreuther 1914 / *printed*

965		HOHENBERG Hutschenreuther 1914 / *printed*
966 967		LUBENZ (Žlutice) H. Reinl after 1846 / *printed*
968		UNTERWEISSBACH H. Schaubach after 1880 / *printed*
969		LANE END Hilditsch & Son after 1830 / *blue*
970		SELB L. Hutschenreuther after 1856—1920 / *printed*
971		HÜTTENSTEINACH Schoenau Bros after 1865 / *blue*
972		BOW W. Duesbury 1760—1776 / *blue*
973		ILMENAU C. Nonne *c.* 1800 / *blue*

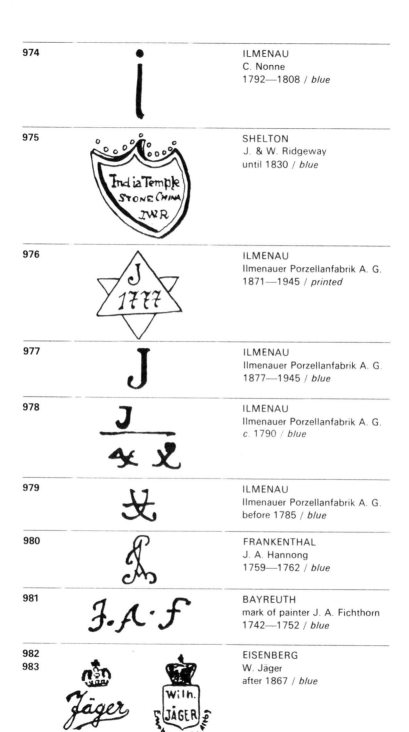

974	ILMENAU C. Nonne 1792—1808 / *blue*
975	SHELTON J. & W. Ridgeway until 1830 / *blue*
976	ILMENAU Ilmenauer Porzellanfabrik A. G. 1871—1945 / *printed*
977	ILMENAU Ilmenauer Porzellanfabrik A. G. 1877—1945 / *blue*
978	ILMENAU Ilmenauer Porzellanfabrik A. G. *c.* 1790 / *blue*
979	ILMENAU Ilmenauer Porzellanfabrik A. G. before 1785 / *blue*
980	FRANKENTHAL J. A. Hannong 1759—1762 / *blue*
981	BAYREUTH mark of painter J. A. Fichthorn 1742—1752 / *blue*
982 983	EISENBERG W. Jäger after 1867 / *blue*

984	J E H F	FRIEDLAND (Frýdlant) J. E. Heintschel after 1869 / *blue*
985		VIENNA J. Goldschneider after 1882 / *blue*
986 987	iH	FRANKENTHAL J. A. Hannong 1759—1762 / *blue*
988		STRASBOURG P. A. Hannong 1783—1784 / *impressed*
989		KÖPPELSDORF J. Hering & Sohn after 1893 / *printed*
990		ILMENAU Ilmenauer Porzellanfabrik A. G. 1871—1945 / *printed*
991		ILMENAU Ilmenauer Porzellanfabrik A. G. 1871—1945 / *printed*
992		VILLEDIEU SUR INDRE J. Lang after 1882 / *printed*
993		PARIS, CLIGNANCOURT J. Moitte 1789—1798 / *blue*

994		FONTAINEBLEAU Jacob Petit after 1834 / *blue*
995		SCHÖNWALD J. N. Müller after 1879 / *blue*
996		ILMENAU Ilmenauer Porzellanfabrik A. G. 1871—1945 / *printed*
997		LIMOGES J. Pouyat after 1842 / *blue*
998 999		ILMENAU Ilmenauer Porzellanfabrik A. G. 1871—1945 / *printed*
1000 1001		KLAUSENBURG (Cluj) "Iris" Porcelain after 1922 / *printed*
1002		VOHENSTRAUSS J. Seltmann after 1910 / *printed*
1003 1004		CHARLOTTENBRUNN (Zofiówka) J. Schachtel after 1859 / *printed*

1005	ITALY New Stone G. RICHARD & C.	MILAN G. Richard & Co. 1870—1873 / *printed*
1006		KLÖSTERLE (Klášterec) M. Weber 1794—1798 / *blue, red*
1007		KLÖSTERLE (Klášterec) Gräfliche Thun'sche Porzellan- fabrik 1804—1830 / *blue, gold*
1008		KLÖSTERLE (Klášterec) M. Weber 1794—1798 / *blue*
1009		KORZEC M. Mezer after 1803 / *red*
1010		KORZEC M. Mezer after 1803 / *blue, impressed*
1011		LAUF F. Krug after 1871 / *printed*
1012		ELBOGEN (Loket) H. Kretschmann *c.* 1900 / *printed*
1013		OBERHOHNDORF F. Kaestner after 1883 / *printed*

1014		KAHLA Porzellanfabrik after 1844 / *printed*
1015		EISENBERG Porzellanfabrik Kalk G. m. b. H. after 1900 / *printed*
1016		FISCHERN (Rybáře) C. Knoll mid-19th cent. / *printed*
1017		FISCHERN (Rybáře) Karlsbader Porzellanfabrik beginning of 20th cent. *printed*
1018		FISCHERN (Rybáře) Karlsbader Porzellanfabrik 1900—1910 / *printed*
1019		FISCHERN (Rybáře) Karlsbader Porzellanfabrik 1st half of 20th cent. / *printed*
1020		FISCHERN (Rybáře) Karlsbader Porzellanfabrik 1939—1945 / *printed*
1021		FISCHERN (Rybáře) Karlsbader Porzellanfabrik c. 1910 / *printed*

1022		FISCHERN (Rybáře) Karlsbader Porzellanfabrik beginning of 20th cent. *printed*
1023		KARLSKRONA Karlskrona Porslinsfabrik after 1918 / *printed*
1024		UPPSALA Karlskrona Porslinsfabrik after 1945 / *printed*
1025		KATZHÜTTE J. W. Hamann 19th cent. / *printed*
1026		KATZHÜTTE Hertwig & Co. after 1945 / *printed*
1027		WORCESTER Kerr & Binns 1852—1862 / *printed*
1028		OHRDRUF Kestner 20th cent / *printed*
1029		MEISSEN Königliche Hofconditorei Warschau 1713—1806 / *various colours*

1030		LANGEWIESEN O. Schlegelmilch after 1842 / *printed*
1031		COPENHAGEN Bing & Grøndahl after 1905 / *printed*
1032		KLENTSCH (Kleneč) A. Schmidt 1835—1889 / *impressed*
1033		WISTRITZ (Bystřice) Krantzberger, Mayer & Purkert after 1911 / *printed*
1034		KONIGSZELT (Jaworzyna Śląska) Porcelain Factory after 1860 / *printed*
1035		KONIGSZELT (Jaworzyna Śląska) Porcelain Factory after 1860 / *printed*
1036		CHODAU (Chodov) J. Hüttner & Co. 1835—1840 / *impressed*
1037		KÖPPELSDORF J. Hering & Sohn after 1893 / *printed*
1038		KORZEC Mérault & Petion 1822 / *red*
1039		KORZEC Mérault & Petion 1830 / *red*

| 1040 | | KORZEC
M. Mezer
beginning of 19th cent. / *red* |

korzec

| 1041
1042 |
 | KORZEC
M. Mezer
beginning of 19th cent. / *red* |

| 1043 | | KORZEC
F. Mezer
1793—1814 / *blue* |

| 1044 | | KORZEC
F. Mezer
1st half of 19th cent. / *gold* |

| 1045 |  | EISENBERG
Porzellanfabrik Kalk G. m. b. H.
after 1900 / *printed* |

| 1046 |  | MEISSEN
Königl. Porzellanmanufaktur
from 1722 / *blue* |

| 1047 |  | MEISSEN
Königl. Porzellanmanufaktur
1723—1724 / *blue* |

| 1048 | | MEISSEN
Königl. Porzellanmanufaktur
1723—1724 / *blue* |

| 1049 | | MEISSEN
Königl. Porzellanmanufaktur
1723—1724 / *blue* |

1050		BERLIN Königl. Porzellanmanufaktur 1823—1832 / *blue*
1051		WALDENBURG (Walbrzych) Krister Porzellanmanufaktur 1831—1945 / *printed*
1052		WALDENBURG (Walbrzych) Krister Porzellanmanufaktur until 1945 / *printed*
1053		BERLIN Königl. Porzellanmanufaktur 1844—1847 / *blue*
1054		BERLIN Königl. Porzellanmanufaktur from 1857 / *blue*
1055		SCHEIBE-ALSBACH A. W. F. Kister after 1837 / *blue*
1056		SCHEIBE-ALSBACH A. W. F. Kister after 1831 / *blue*
1057		WALDENBURG (Walbrzych) Krister Porzellanmanufaktur after 1900 / *blue*
1058 **1059**		WALDENBURG (Walbrzych) Krister Porzellanmanufaktur after 1831 / *blue*
1060		BERLIN Königl. Porzellanmanufaktur 1837—1844 / *blue*

1061	**K P M** / **W**	WALDENBURG (Walbrzych) Krister Porzellanmanufaktur 19th cent. / *blue*
1062		SELB Krautheim & Adelberg after 1884 / *printed*
1063		SELB Krautheim & Adelberg after 1884 / *printed*
1064		WISTRITZ (Bystřice) Krantzberger, Mayer & Purkert after 1911 / *printed*
1065		LANDSTUHL Krister Porzellanmanufaktur after 1952 / *printed*
1066		KRONACH Stockhardt & Schmidt-Eckert after 1912 / *printed*
1067 1068		BLANKENHAIN E. Krüger after 1847 / *printed*
1069		TIEFENFURTH (Parowa) K. Steinmann G. m. b. H. 1883—1932 / *printed*

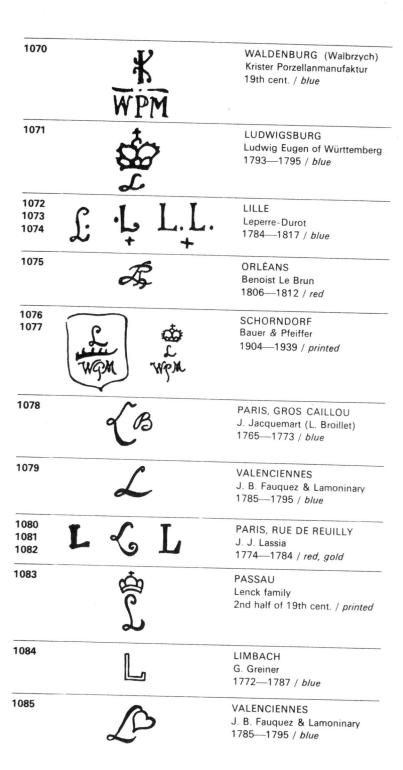

1070	WALDENBURG (Walbrzych) Krister Porzellanmanufaktur 19th cent. / *blue*
1071	LUDWIGSBURG Ludwig Eugen of Württemberg 1793—1795 / *blue*
1072 **1073** **1074**	LILLE Leperre-Durot 1784—1817 / *blue*
1075	ORLÉANS Benoist Le Brun 1806—1812 / *red*
1076 **1077**	SCHORNDORF Bauer & Pfeiffer 1904—1939 / *printed*
1078	PARIS, GROS CAILLOU J. Jacquemart (L. Broillet) 1765—1773 / *blue*
1079	VALENCIENNES J. B. Fauquez & Lamoninary 1785—1795 / *blue*
1080 **1081** **1082**	PARIS, RUE DE REUILLY J. J. Lassia 1774—1784 / *red, gold*
1083	PASSAU Lenck family 2nd half of 19th cent. / *printed*
1084	LIMBACH G. Greiner 1772—1787 / *blue*
1085	VALENCIENNES J. B. Fauquez & Lamoninary 1785—1795 / *blue*

1086 1087		LETTIN H. Baensch 1858—1945 / *printed*

1088		LUDWIGSBURG Ludwig Eugen of Württemberg 1793—1795 / *blue*

1089		LANGEWIESEN O. Schlegelmilch after 1892 / *printed*

1090	LAC	LISBON J. J. Paszoa after 1870 / *printed*

1091	Lange BAVARIA	KRUMMENNAAB H. Lange & Co. after 1934 / *printed*

1092 1093	L·B ℬ	LUXEMBOURG Bloch Sept Fontaines 19th cent. / *blue*

1094 1095	ℬ B.L	LUXEMBOURG Bloch Sept Fontaines 19th cent. / *blue*

1096	ℬ 7h 1768	LASSAY Comte de Lauraguais-Brancas 1763—1768 / *blue, various colours*

1097	B	LUXEMBOURG Bloch Sept Fontaines 19th cent. / *blue, various colours*

1098	ℬ	LUXEMBOURG Bloch Sept Fontaines 19th cent. / *blue*

1099	LUXEMBOURG Bloch Sept Fontaines 19th cent. / *impressed*
1100 **1101**	LASSAY Comte de Lauraguais-Brancas 1763—1768 / *incised*
1102	LIMBACH G. Greiner 1762—1787 / *incised*
1103	LIMBACH G. Greiner 1762—1787 / *blue*
1104	ORLÉANS Benoist Le Brun 1806—1812 / *blue*
1105 **1106**	BRUSSELS L. Cretté 1791—1803 / *blue*
1107	BRUSSELS L. Cretté 1791—1803 / *blue*
1108	BRUSSELS L. Cretté 1791—1803 / *blue*
1109	BRUSSELS L. Cretté 1791—1803 / *blue*
1110	DERBY Royal Crown Porcelain Co. from 1876 / *printed*

1111	LETTIN H. Baensch after 1858 / *blue*
1112	LETTIN Porzellanfabrik after 1945 / *printed*
1113 **1114** 	LETTIN H. Baensch after 1858 / *blue*
1115	KAHLA C. A. Lehmann & Sohn after 1895 / *printed*
1116	LICHTE Heubach Bros after 1820 / *blue*
1117	SCHLAGGENWALD (Slavkov) J. Lippert & A. Haas 1830—1846 / *impressed*
1118	SELB L. Hutschenreuther after 1920—1938 / *printed*
1119 	ALT-ROHLAU (Stará Role) J. Schneider & Co. after 1904 / *blue*

1120 	LILLE Leperre-Durot 1784—1817 / *blue, red, gold*
1121	LIMBACH Greiner family 1882 / *printed*
1122 **1123** 	LIMBACH Greiner family 1882 / *printed*
1124	LIMOGES Royal Porcelain Factory J. F. Alluaud 1788—1793 / *blue*
1125	LIMOGES Royal Porcelain Factory 1784—1796 / *blue, red, gold*
1126	LIMOGES J. Pouyat after 1842 / *green*
1127	LIMBACH G. Greiner 1772—1787 / *blue*
1128	LIMBACH G. Greiner 1772—1787 / *blue*

1129	*porcelaine royalle de Limoges* C D	LIMOGES Royal Porcelain Factory Comte d'Artois 1771 —1784 / *blue, red, gold, incised*
1130	LIMOGES B & Cie FRANCE	LIMOGES H. A. Balleroy Frères 19th cent. / *blue*
1131	LIMOGES J. B & Cie FRANCE	LIMOGES J. Balleroy & Co. 19th cent. / *blue*
1132	B & C° LIMOGES (FRANCE)	LIMOGES L. Bernardaux & Co. after 1863 / *blue*
1133	B & Co LIMOGES FRANCE	LIMOGES L. Bernardaux & Co. after 1863 / *printed*
1134	LIMOGES BRP FRANCE	LIMOGES Beulé, Reboisson & Parot 19th cent. / *blue, printed*
1135	PORCELAINE ARTISTIQUE DE LIMOGES BARBOTINE F. M. GRAND FEU	LIMOGES Fontanille & Marraud after 1925 / *printed*
1136	PORCELAINE ARTISTIQUE F. M. LIMOGES FRANCE MADE IN F LIMOGES M FRANCE	LIMOGES Fontanille & Marraud 19th cent. / *printed*
1137	FRANCE M DE M LIMOGES	LIMOGES Granger & Co. 19th cent. / *printed*

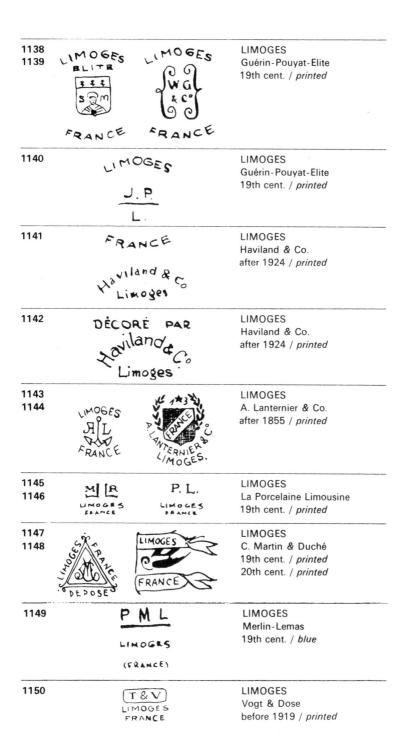

1138 1139	LIMOGES Guérin-Pouyat-Elite 19th cent. / printed
1140	LIMOGES Guérin-Pouyat-Elite 19th cent. / printed
1141	LIMOGES Haviland & Co. after 1924 / printed
1142	LIMOGES Haviland & Co. after 1924 / printed
1143 1144	LIMOGES A. Lanternier & Co. after 1855 / printed
1145 1146	LIMOGES La Porcelaine Limousine 19th cent. / printed
1147 1148	LIMOGES C. Martin & Duché 19th cent. / printed 20th cent. / printed
1149	LIMOGES Merlin-Lemas 19th cent. / blue
1150	LIMOGES Vogt & Dose before 1919 / printed

1151	R & C? LIMOGES FRANCE	LIMOGES Raynaud & Co. 1919 / *printed*
1152		LIMOGES Raynaud & Co. after 1919 / *printed*
1153		LIMOGES Rousset & Guillerot 20th cent. / *printed*
1154		LIMOGES Societé Porcelainière de Limoges 20th cent. / *printed*
1155		LIMOGES Fabrique de Porcelaines Blanches & Décorées Anciens Ets. after 1908 / *printed*
1156		LIMOGES Touze, Lemaître Frères & Blancher 19th cent. / *printed*
1157 **1158**		LIMOGES Union Céramique 19th cent. / *printed*
1159 **1160**		LIMOGES Union Limousine after 1908 / *printed*
1161		LIMOGES A. Vignaud after 1911 / *printed*

1162		LIMOGES Villegoureix 19th cent. / *printed*
1163		LIMOGES A. Vignaud after 1911 / *blue*
1164		LIMOGES Villegoureix 19th cent. / *printed*
1165		SCHLAGGENWALD (Slavkov) J. Lippert & A. Haas 1830—1846 / *impressed*
1166		SCHLAGGENWALD (Slavkov) J. Lippert & A. Haas 1830—1846 / *printed*
1167	LTSBDA 1793	LISBON J. M. Perreira end of 18th cent. / *gold, red*
1168		LIMOGES Manuf. de Porcelaines Ets. Legrand 19th cent. / *printed*
1169		LIMBACH G. Greiner 1772—1787 / *blue*
1170 **1171**		VINCENNES Royal Porcelain Factory 1740—1752 / *blue*
1172		VINCENNES Royal Porcelain Factory 1740—1752 / *blue*

1173		VINCENNES Royal Porcelain Factory 1740—1752 / *blue*
1174		VINCENNES Royal Porcelain Factory 1740—1752 / *gold*
1175		VINCENNES Royal Porcelain Factory 1753—1756 / *blue*
1176		VINCENNES Royal Porcelain Factory 1754 / *blue*
1177		VINCENNES Royal Porcelain Factory 1755 / *blue*
1178		VINCENNES Royal Porcelain Factory 1740—1752 / *blue*
1179		VINCENNES Royal Porcelain Factory 1753—1756 / *blue*
1180		SÈVRES Royal Porcelain Factory 1778 / *blue, various colours*
1181		SÈVRES Royal Porcelain Factory (hard-paste) 1756 / *blue, various colours*

1182		SÈVRES Royal Porcelain Factory (hard-paste) 1769—1793 / *blue, various colours*
1183		COALPORT imitation of Sèvres mark 1860—1880 / *blue*
1184		FOECY L. Lourioux 19th cent. / *printed*
1185		FENTON E. Hughes after 1883 / *printed*
1186		LONGTON Hammersley & Co. *c.* 1900 / *printed*
1187	A Trefle From LOWESTOFT	LOWESTOFT R. Allen after 1802 / *blue*
1188	James & Mary Curtis Lowestoft	LOWESTOFT James & Mary Curtis after 1757—1771 / *black*
1189		VINCENNES Louis Philippe, duc de Chartres 1777—1788 / *blue*
1190		PARIS, RUE AMELOT under the aegis of Louis Philippe, duc d'Orléans 1786—1793 / *blue*

1191		ORLÉANS Benoist Le Brun 1806—1812 / *red*
1192		VINCENNES Louis Philippe, duc de Chartres 1777—1788 / *blue*
1193		BORDEAUX Lahens & Rateau after 1819 / *blue*
1194		LA SEYNIE Marquis de Beaupoil & Co. 1774—1789 / *blue, red*
1195		LA SEYNIE E. Baignol 1789—1856 / *blue, red*
1196		LA SEYNIE E. Baignol 1789—1856 / *blue, red*
1197		VENDRENNES M. Lozelet after 1800 / *blue*
1198		LUBARTÓW Count H. Lubieński 1840—1850 / *impressed*
1199		LUBARTÓW Count H. Lubieński 1840—1850 / *impressed*
1200		LUBARTÓW Count H. Lubieński 1840—1850 / *impressed*
1201		PODERSAM (Podbořany) Porzellanfabrik "Alp" G. m. b. H. 1920—1941 / *printed*

1202		SCHORNDORF Bauer & Pfeiffer 1904—1939 / *printed*
1203		VINOVO G. Lormello 1815—1820 / *blue*
1204		VALENCIENNES Lamoninary 1800—1810 / *blue, red, brown,* *black*
1205		VALENCIENNES Lamoninary 1800—1810 / *blue, red, brown,* *black*
1206		SCHORNDORF Bauer & Pfeiffer 1904—1939 / *printed*
1207		SCHORNDORF Bauer & Pfeiffer 1904—1939 / *printed*
1208		FLORENCE Francesco II Medici 1578—1587 / *blue*
1209		VOLKSTEDT-RUDOLSTADT G. H. Macheleid 1760—1762 / *violet*
1210		PARIS, CLIGNANCOURT Fabrique de Monsieur 1775—1793 / *red*

1211 1212		PARIS, CLIGNANCOURT J. Moitte 1793—1798 / *blue*
1213		SCHWARZA-SAALBAHN E. & A. Müller after 1890 / *blue*
1214 1215		STOKE-ON-TRENT T. Minton 1793—1835 / *various colours,* *gold*
1216		HANLEY Booths & Colclough Ltd. 20th cent. / *printed*
1217	M A	CHANTILLY M. Aron Père after 1845 / *printed*
1218		MAYERHÖFEN Benedikt Bros 1883—1918 / *printed*
1219		MÄBENDORF Mathes & Ebel after 1882 / *printed*
1220 1221		MÄBENDORF Mathes & Ebel after 1882 / *printed*
1222 1223	MB	MARIEBERG P. Berthevin 1766—1769 / *incised*
1224		MARIEBERG P. Berthevin 1766—1769 / *incised*

1225	MARIEBERG H. Sten and J. Dortu 1777—1778 / *blue*
1226	ELGERSBURG E. & F. C. Arnoldi after 1808 / *blue*
1227	HOHENBERG C. M. Hutschenreuther 1860 / *impressed*
1228 **1229**	LA MONCLOA Royal Porcelain Factory 1817—1850 / *red*
1230	MEHUN-SUR-YÈVRE Pillivuyt & Co. after 1853 / *blue*
1231	EICHWALD (Dubi) Dr Widera & Co.; imitation of Meissen with onion pattern 19th—20th cent. / *blue*
1232	KÖNITZ Metzel Bros after 1909 / *blue*
1233	LUBAU (Hlubany) Martin Bros after 1874 / *blue*
1234	KÖNITZ Metzel Bros 1909—1950 / *blue*
1235	KÖNITZ Metzel Bros 1909—1950 / *blue*

1236		MILAN S. Richard after 1883 / *blue*
1237		DELFT Ary de Milde end of 17th cent. / *impressed*
1238 **1239**		STOKE-ON-TRENT T. Minton and successors 1941 / *printed*
1240		HANLEY "Blue Mist" 20th cent. / *printed*
1241 **1242**		MITTERTEICH Porzellanfabrik after 1917 / *printed*
1243		MITTERTEICH Porzellanfabrik after 1917 / *printed*
1244		SÈVRES period of the Consulate 1803—1804 / *red, printed*

1245		ILMENAU Metzler Bros & Ortloff after 1875 / *blue*
1246		PARIS, RUE AMELOT Manufacture du duc d'Orléans (J. B. Outrequin) 1786—1793 / *red, gold*
1247		MOABIT M. Schuman & Sohn 1835 / *blue*
1248	M:OL.	OUDE LOOSDRECHT J. de Mol 1771—1784 / *incised*
1249	M:OL.	OUDE LOOSDRECHT J. de Mol 1771—1784 / *black, various colours*
1250	M:ol	OUDE LOOSDRECHT J. de Mol 1771—1784 / *red, various colours*
1251	M.O.L ✳	OUDE LOOSDRECHT Manufacture Oude Loosdrecht after 1784 / *blue, gold*
1252	M:OL.	OUDE LOOSDRECHT J. de Mol 1771—1784 / *impressed*
1253	Mol Lm3	OUDE LOOSDRECHT J. de Mol 1771—1784 / *violet*
1254	M.ol Nº10	OUDE LOOSDRECHT J. de Mol 1771—1784 / *blue, impressed*
1255	M:ol	OUDE LOOSDRECHT J. de Mol 1771—1784 / *impressed*

1256	M:ᴀoL	OUDE LOOSDRECHT J. de Mol 1771—1784 / *blue*
1257	M·OL L 27	OUDE LOOSDRECHT J. de Mol 1771—1784 / *gold, violet*
1258	M: o: L 87	OUDE LOOSDRECHT Manufacture Oude Loosdrecht after 1784 / *blue*
1259	M o Moitte	PARIS, CLIGNANCOURT J. Moitte 1793—1798 / *blue*
1260 **1261**	M⚒O I M&O	ILMENAU Metzler Bros & Ortloff after 1875 / *printed*
1262	MONCLOA	LA MONCLOA Royal Porcelain Factory 1817—1850 / *impressed*
1263	MOSA MAASTRICHT (FABRIEKSMERK)	MAASTRICHT L. Regout & Zonen after 1883 / *printed*
1264	PM Moschendorf BAVARIA	HOF-MOSCHENDORF O. Reinecke after 1878 / *printed*
1265 **1266**	MP· MP	ETIOLLES J. B. Monier & D. Pellevé 1768—1770 / *incised*
1267	M.P.M.	MEISSEN Meissener Porzellanmanufaktur after 1722 / *blue*

1268

MAASTRICHT
Manufaktur Porselein Mosa
after 1883 / *printed*

1269

BAYREUTH
S. P. Meyer
after 1900 / *printed*

1270

VOLKSTEDT-RUDOLSTADT
Müller & Co.
after 1907 / *printed*

1271

VOLOKITINO
A. Miklaszewski
1820—1864 / *printed*

1272
1273

NAPLES
Royal Porcelain Factory
1771—1834 / *blue, impressed*

1274
1275

NAPLES
Royal Porcelain Factory
1771—1834 / *blue, impressed*

1276

NAPLES
Royal Porcelain Factory
1771—1834 / *blue*

1277

SÈVRES
2nd Empire period
1852—1870 / *red*

1278

DOCCIA
casts of Capodimonte models
1850—1903 / *blue*

1279 **1280**	*N* *N*	LE NOVE Antonibon family end of 18th—19th cent. *incised*
1281	*N*	NIDERVILLER A. P. de Custine—C. F. Lanfrey 1780—1800 / *black*
1282	*N*	SHELTON, NEW HALL New Hall China Factory 1781—1825 / *blue*
1283 **1284**	N ▌	ALT-HALDENSLEBEN Nathusius after 1826 / *blue*
1285	👑 **N**	VOLKSTEDT-RUDOLSTADT E. Bohne & Söhne 1854—1900 / *blue*
1286	👑 *ÆV*	VOLKSTEDT-RUDOLSTADT K. Ens after 1898 / *blue*
1287	*N=36=* **w**	MEISSEN Königliche Porzellanmanufaktur numbered white porcelain to no. 68 before 1725 / *blue*
1288	*N 198* ✳ **TTL**	CHELSEA 19th cent. / *impressed*
1289	*Nantgarv*	NANTGARW W. Billingsley & S. Walker 1813—1822 / *blue*
1290	NANTGARW.	NANTGARW W. Billingsley & S. Walker 1813—1822 / *impressed*

1291	**NAST.**	PARIS, RUE POPINCOURT J. N. H. Nast 1782—1835 / *red, gold*
1292	**NAST A PARIS**	PARIS, RUE POPINCOURT J. N. H. Nast 1782—1835 / *red, gold*
1293		COALPORT Coalport, Nantgarw, Swansea 1861 / *gold*
1294		SHELTON, NEW HALL Hollins & Warburton *c.* 1800 / *printed*
1295		VOLKSTEDT-RUDOLSTADT K. Ens after 1898 / *blue*
1296		LUNÉVILLE P. L. Cyfflé 1769—1780 / *blue*
1297 1298	**N.G.** **N.G.F.**	GIESSHÜBEL (Kysibl) W. von Neuberg 1847—1902 / *impressed*
1299	*Nider*	NIDERVILLER A. P. de Custine—C. F. Lanfrey 1780—1800 / *black*
1300	**NIDERVILLER**	NIDERVILLER A. P. de Custine—C. F. Lanfrey end of 18th cent. / *impressed*
1301	*Niderviller*	NIDERVILLER A. P. de Custine—C. F. Lanfrey 1780—1800 / *black*

1302	Nove ✳	LE NOVE Antonibon family from 1781 / *gold*
1303	∂ʌoN Nove	LE NOVE Antonibon family 1763—1773 / *relief*
1304	·Nove	LE NOVE Antonibon family from 1781 / *incised*
1305	G.B, NOVE	LE NOVE G. Baroni 1802—1825 / *various colours*
1306	NOVE ✳	LE NOVE G. Baroni 1802—1825 / *impressed*
1307	No:ue 🌺 G·B·A·B:	LE NOVE G. B. Antonibon from 1762 / *gold, various colours*
1308	Houe▲ Antonio Bon	LE NOVE Antonibon family 1762—1802 / *red*
1309	Fabbrica Baroni Nove.	LE NOVE G. Baroni 1802—1825 / *blue*

1310	**G B** **NOVE**	LE NOVE G. Baroni 1802—1825 / *blue*
1311		NOVI SAD Fabrika porculana after 1922 / *printed*
1312		ALT-ROHLAU (Stará Role) A. Nowotny 1838—1884 / *impressed*
1313	**N&R**	ILMENAU C. Nonne & K. Roesch 1808—1871 / *printed*
1314	**.N.S.**	OTTWEILER Prince of Nassau-Saarbrücken 1763—1794 / *blue, gold*
1315	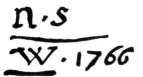	OTTWEILER Prince of Nassau-Saarbrücken (manager H. Wagner) 1766 / *incised*
1316		ALT-ROHLAU (Stará Role) O. & E. Gutherz 1899—1918 / *printed*
1317		OHRDRUF Baehr & Proeschild after 1871 / *printed*
1318		OISSEL La Céramique "Normande" 20th cent. / *printed*

1319		ORLÉANS G. d'Aureaubert 1753—1783 / *blue*
1320		BOURG LA REINE J. Jullien & S. Jacques 1773—1804 / *printed*
1321		TRIPTIS Triptis A. G. Porzellanfabrik after 1891/*printed*
1322		TRIPTIS Triptis A. G. Porzellanfabrik after 1891 / *printed*
1323 **1324**		PRAGUE K. Kriegel & Co. after 1837 / *impressed*
1325		KORZEC Merault & Petion 1815—1929 / *blue*
1326		KORZEC Petion 1815—1829 / *blue, red, gold,* *impressed*
1327		LORIENT Charey, Sauvageau & Hervé *c.* 1800 / *blue*
1328 **1329**		PINXTON W. Billingsley & J. Coke 1796—1813 / *red*
1330		ETIOLLES D. Pellevé 1768—1770 / *incised*
1331		SCHMIEDEBERG (Kowary) Pohl Bros after 1871 / *blue*

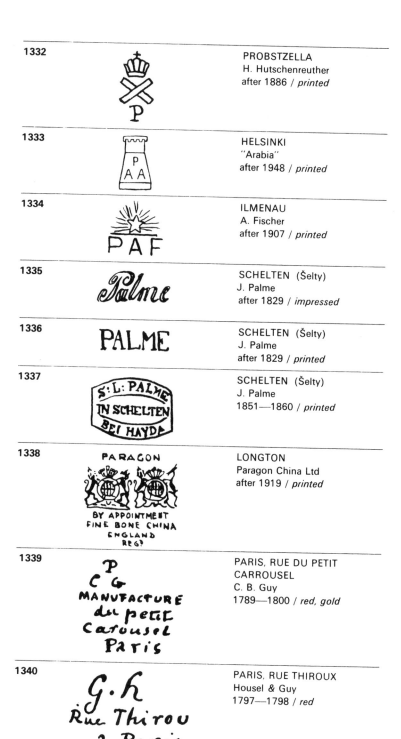

1332	PROBSTZELLA H. Hutschenreuther after 1886 / *printed*
1333	HELSINKI "Arabia" after 1948 / *printed*
1334	ILMENAU A. Fischer after 1907 / *printed*
1335	SCHELTEN (Šelty) J. Palme after 1829 / *impressed*
1336	SCHELTEN (Šelty) J. Palme after 1829 / *printed*
1337	SCHELTEN (Šelty) J. Palme 1851—1860 / *printed*
1338	LONGTON Paragon China Ltd after 1919 / *printed*
1339	PARIS, RUE DU PETIT CARROUSEL C. B. Guy 1789—1800 / *red, gold*
1340	PARIS, RUE THIROUX Housel & Guy 1797—1798 / *red*

1341	MANUFRE de MGR le Duc d'angouléme a Paris	PARIS, RUE DE BONDY Manufacture du duc d'Angoulême 1781—1793 / *red*
1342	MANUFRᵉ de MM Guerhard et Dihla Paris	PARIS, RUE DE BONDY J. Dihl & Guerhard 1793—1817 / *red*
1343	MANUFRᵉ DE PORCELAINE DU Cᵉⁿ NAST A PARIS	PARIS, RUE POPINCOURT J. N. H. Nast 1782—1835 / *incised*
1344	PB	PARIS, RUE DE CRUSSOL C. Potter & Blancheron 1792—beginning of 19th cent. *blue*
1345	PB	IRÚN Luso Espanola de Porcelanas, Fabrica de Bidosa after 1935 / *printed*
1346	(FPC)	CREIDLITZ Porzellanfabrik A. G. after 1907 / *printed*
1347	C P G	PARIS, RUE DU PETIT CARROUSEL C. B. Guy 1789—1800 / *red, gold*
1348	P	GOTHA E. Pfeffer after 1892 / *printed*
1349	(P/G)	GEHREN Porzellanfabrik Günthersfeld A. G. after 1884 / *printed*
1350	P H	STRASBOURG Paul A. Hannong 1751—1754 / *incised, blue*

1351	**PH**	STRASBOURG Paul A. Hannong 1751—1754 / *impressed*
1352		STRASBOURG (HAGENAU) Pierre A. Hannong (Hagenau factory) 1783—1784 / *blue*
1353		STRASBOURG (HAGENAU) Pierre A. Hannong (Hagenau factory) 1783—1784 / *incised*
1354 1355	**PHF** **PH** **F**	FRANKENTHAL Paul A. Hannong 1755—1759 / *impressed*
1356	PICKMAN Y.CA. CHINA OPACA SEVILLA	SEVILLE "La Cartuja"; de Aponte, Pickmann & Co. after 1867 / *printed*
1357	PICKMANN Y C CHINA OPACA	SEVILLE "La Cartuja"; de Aponte, Pickmann & Co. after 1867 / *printed*
1358	P&F France **C. H. PILLIVUYT** *& Cie Paris.* PARIS. FOECY. MEHUN.	FOËCY C. H. Pillivuyt 2nd half of 19th cent. / *printed*
1359	PILIVITE PORCELAINES A FEU PILLIVUYT&Cⁱᵉ MEHUN FRANCE	MEHUN-SUR-YÈVRE C. H. Pillivuyt after 1852 / *printed*
1360	PINK Vogue BONE CHINA MADE IN ENGLAND	HANLEY Booths & Colclough Ltd 19th cent. / *printed*

1361		PIRKENHAMMER (Březová) "Epiag" 1918—1938 / *printed*
1362	P R	KORZEC Petion 1815—1828 / *red*
1363		PARIS, RUE AMELOT Manufacture du duc d'Orléans 1786—1793 / *blue*
1364		KRUMMENNAAB Illinger & Co. after 1931 / *printed*
1365		KALTENHOF (Oblanov) J. Dietel 1918—1938 / *printed*
1366	P L	STADTLENGSFELD Porzellanfabrik A. G. after 1889 / *printed*
1367		PLANKENHAMMER Fross Bros after 1908 / *printed*
1368		LONGTON R. H. Plant & Co. after 1880 / *printed*
1369		SCHLACKENWERTH (Ostrov) Pfeiffer & Löwenstein 20th cent. / *printed*
1370	PLS	SCHLACKENWERTH (Ostrov) Pfeiffer & Löwenstein 20th cent. / *printed*

1371		HOF MOSCHENDORF O. Reinecke after 1878 / *printed*
1372		POSCHETZAU (Božičany) Maier & Co. 1938—1945 / *printed*
1373		OBERKOTZAU Neuerer K. G. after 1943 / *printed*
1374		PONTENX De Rosly 1779—1790 / *blue*
1375		POTSCHAPPEL C. Thieme after 1872 / *printed*
1376		POTSCHAPPEL C. Thieme after 1872 / *printed*
1377		PARIS, RUE DE CRUSSOL Manufacture du prince de Galles (C. Potter) 1789—1792 / *blue*
1378		FREIWALDAU (Gozdnica) H. Schmidt 20th cent. / *printed*

1379		PLANKENHAMMER Porzellanfabrik after 1908 / *printed*
1380 **1381**	PRAG K&C PRAG	PRAGUE K. Kriegel & Co. after 1837 / *impressed*
1382	Prag	PRAGUE K. Kriegel & Co. after 1837 / *impressed*
1383	P & S	CHODAU (Chodov) Portheim & Sohn *c.* 1870 / *impressed*
1384		POTSCHAPPEL C. Thieme after 1872 / *blue*
1385	P S	SORAU (Žary) C. & E. Carstens after 1918 / *printed*
1386	BST A·G	STADTLENGSFELD Porzellanfabrik A. G. after 1889 / *printed*
1387	Puls	SCHLACKENWERTH (Ostrov) Pfeiffer & Löwenstein 1st half of 20th cent. / *printed*
1388	PR	FRANKENTHAL P. van Recum 1795 / *blue*
1389	P.Y.C 12	SEVILLE "La Cartuja"; de Aponte, Pickmann & Co. after 1867 / *printed*

1390	ZWEIBRÜCKEN, GUTENBRUNN Christian IV of Pfalz- Zweibrücken 1768—1775 / *blue*
1391	LONGTON Shore & Coggins Ltd 19th cent. / *printed*
1392	ALT-ROHLAU (Stará Role) A. Nowotny 1838—1884 / *impressed*
1393 **1394**	LUDWIGSBURG Fridericus Rex 1806—1816 / *red, gold*
1395	FRANKENTHAL P. van Recum 1797—1799 / *blue*
1396	RAUENSTEIN Greiner Bros after 1783 / *blue*
1397	VOLKSTEDT-RUDOLSTADT Holzapfel & Greiner 1799—1817 / *blue*
1398	VOLKSTEDT-RUDOLSTADT Holzapfel & Greiner 1799—1817 / *blue*
1399	GOTHA W. von Rothberg 1757—1783 / *blue*
1400	GOTHA C. Schultz, Gabel & Brehm 1783—1805 / *blue*

1401 **1402**		MARSEILLE J. G. Robert 1773—1793 / *blue, black,* *red, gold*
1403		RÖRSTRAND Porcelain Factory 20th cent. / *blue*
1404		MILAN G. Richard 1842—1860 / *blue*
1405		MILAN G. Richard *c.* 1850 / *blue*
1406		MILAN G. Richard 1870 / *blue*
1407		MILAN G. Richard 1860—1870 / *blue*
1408		MILAN G. Richard *c.* 1870 / *blue*
1409 **1410**		SAINT UZE G. Revol Père & Fils after 1780 / *blue*
1411		MITTERTEICH J. Rieber after 1868 / *printed*

1412

CAMBRIDGE
Ivory

MITTERTEICH
J. Rieber
after 1868 / *printed*

1413

ROSCHÜTZ
Unger & Schilde
1821 / *printed*

1414

ROSCHÜTZ
Unger & Schilde and successors
20th cent. / *printed*

1415

SCHMIEDEBERG (Kowary)
Pohl Bros
after 1871 / *printed*

1416

FENTON
S. Radford Ltd
after 1883 / *printed*

1417

FENTON
S. Radford Ltd
after 1883 / *printed*

1418

RADNOR
BONE CHINA
ENGLAND

LONGTON
Hall Bros Ltd
after 1947 / *printed*

1419

R✕C.

SELB
Rosenthal A. G.
1891—1907 / *printed*

1420		STOKE-ON-TRENT Mintons & Hollins 1867 / *printed*
1421		TURIN G. G. Rosetti after 1742 / *blue*
1422 **1423**		SÈVRES First Republic period 1793—1800 / *blue*
1424		FRANKENTHAL J. N. van Recum 1797—1799 / *blue*
1425		CHODAU (Chodov) Richter, Falke & Hahn after 1882 / *printed*
1426		CHODAU (Chodov) Richter, Falke & Hahn 1918—1945 / *printed*
1427		CHODAU (Chodov) Richter, Falke & Hahn 1918—1945 / *printed*
1428		LA MONCLOA Ferdinand VII of Spain 1817—1850 / *blue*
1429		EISENBERG F. A. Reinecke after 1796 / *blue*

1430	*R-g*	GOTHA C. Schultz & Co. 1783—1805 / *blue*
1431	**G. R.**	MILAN G. Richard 1860 / *blue*
1432 **1433**	**G. R.** **R.**	MILAN G. Richard 1842 / *blue*
1434	LA MIGLIOR QUALITA R G M	DOCCIA G. Richard after 1896 / *printed*
1435	*R∕n*	RAUENSTEIN Greiner Bros 1783—19th cent. / *blue,* *impressed*
1436	G.RICHARD SON BARONA	MILAN G. Richard 1847 / *printed*
1437	JULIUS RICHARD & C S. CRISTOFORO	MILAN G. Richard 1850—1860 / *printed*
1438	RICHARD CERAMICA	MILAN G. Richard 1885 / *printed*
1439	G. Richard	MILAN G. Richard 1868—1881 / *printed*
1440	OPAQUE MILAN RICHARD	MILAN G. Richard 1883 / *printed*

1441		SHELTON J. & W. Ridgeway after 1853 / *printed*
1442		GRÜNLAS R. Kampf after 1911 / *printed*
1443		SELB L. Hutschenreuther after 1856 / *printed*
1444		RAUENSTEIN Greiner Bros 1800—1850 / *blue*
1445		RAUENSTEIN Greiner Bros after 1850 / *blue*
1446	ROHLAU	ALT-ROHLAU (Stará Role) A. Nowotny 1838—1884 / *printed*
1447	*Rolaü*	ALT-ROHLAU (Stará Role) A. Nowotny 1838—1884 / *impressed*
1448	**JOHN ROSE & Cⁱᵉ** **COLE BROOK DALE** **1850.**	COALPORT J. Rose & Co. c. 1850 / *printed*
1449		SELB Rosenthal A. G. after 1908 / *printed*
1450		KRONACH Rosenthal & Co. 1933—1953 / *printed*

1451		SELB Rosenthal A. G. after 1867 / *printed*
1452		ROSSLAU H. Schomburg & Söhne 19th cent. / *printed*
1453		RÖRSTRAND Duke Charles after 1809 / *blue*
1454		RÖRSTRAND Porcelain Factory 1838—1840 / *impressed*
1455		RÖRSTRAND Porcelain Factory mid-19th cent. / *printed*
1456		RÖRSTRAND Porcelain Factory 1852 / *blue, gold*
1457		RÖRSTRAND Porcelain Factory 1857—1860 / *brown*
1458		RÖRSTRAND Porcelain Factory from 1870 / *various colours*

1459		GRÜNLAS R. Kampf from 1911 / *printed*
1460		MANNHEIM Rheinische Porzellanfabrik · after 1910 / *printed*
1461 **1462**		SUHL E. Schlegelmilch after 1861 / *printed*
1463 **1464**		TILLOWITZ (Tulowice) R. Schlegelmilch after 1869 / *printed*
1465		FENTON S. Radford Ltd after 1883 / *printed*
1466		TURIN G. G. Rosetti mid-18th cent. / *blue*
1467		SCHORNDORF C. M. Bauer & Pfeiffer 1904 / *printed*
1468	ROYAL-STONE G. RICHARD & C.	MILAN G. Richard 1870—1873 / *printed*

1469		ROZENBURG Porcelain Factory 1885—1905 / *printed*
1470 **1471**	$\int$ $\int$	SCHLAGGENWALD (Slavkov) J. J. Paulus — L. Greiner 1793—1812 / *blue*
1472	$\mathcal{O.}$	SCHLAGGENWALD (Slavkov) J. J. Lippert & V. Haas 1810—1820 / *gold*
1473	$\mathcal{S}$	SCHLAGGENWALD (Slavkov) J. J. Lippert & V. Haas 1810—1820 / *blue*
1474	$\mathcal{S}$	SCHLAGGENWALD (Slavkov) J. J. Lippert & V. Haas 1810—1820 / *impressed*
1475 **1476**	**S** *S*	PARIS, RUE DE LA ROQUETTE Souroux after 1773 / *blue, red*
1477	*S*	CAUGHLEY T. Turner after 1783 / *blue*
1478 **1479**	**S** $\cancel{S}$	SCHNEY E. Liebmann after 1800 / *blue*
1480	$\cancel{S}$	SCHEIBE-ALSBACH A. W. F. Kister after 1834 / *blue*
1481		SAINT VALLIER M. Montagne after 1830 / *printed*

1482		GOTHA Simson Bros after 1883 / *printed*
1483		KÖPPELSDORF-NORD Swaine & Co. after 1854 / *printed*
1484		SITZENDORF Voigt Bros after 1856 / *printed*
1485		SELB Staatliche Porzellanmanufaktur Berlin after 1763 / *blue*
1486 **1487**		TIEFENFURTH (Parowa) P. Donath after 1883 / *printed*
1488		SAINT AMAND LES EAUX J. B. Fauquez end of 18th cent. / *blue*
1489		LONGTON Salisbury China end of 19th cent. / *printed*
1490	SALOPIAN.	LONGTON Salopian Warehouse after 1783 / *printed*
1491	SALOPIAN	CAUGHLEY T. Turner, Salopian China after 1783 / *printed*

1492 	SARGADELOS L. de la Riva & Co. after 1867 / *printed*
1493	FRAUREUTH Porzellanfabrik after 1866 / *printed*
1494 	SAINT CLOUD P. Chicaneau *c.* 1677 / *blue*
1495 **1496** 	SCHWARZENBACH O. Schaller & Co. after 1882 / *printed*
1497	ARZBERG C. Schumann after 1881 / *printed*
1498	SCHWARZENHAMMER Schumann & Schreider after 1905 / *printed*
1499 	WALLENDORF H. Schaubach after 1926 / *printed*

1500 **1501**		SCHIRNDING Porzellanfabrik after 1907 / *printed*
1502		SCHIRNDING Porzellanfabrik after 1907 / *printed*
1503		SCHLAGGENWALD (Slavkov) J. Lippert & A. Haas 1830—1846 / *printed*
1504		SCHLAGGENWALD (Slavkov) A. Haas 1843—1867 / *printed*
1505	SCHLAGGENWALD	SCHLAGGENWALD (Slavkov) Haas & Czjizek after 1867 / *printed*
1506		SCHLAGGENWALD (Slavkov) J. Lippert & A. Haas 1830—1846 / *impressed*
1507		SCHLAGGENWALD (Slavkov) Haas & Czjizek 1918—1938 / *printed*
1508 **1509**		SCHLAGGENWALD (Slavkov) Haas & Czjizek 20th cent. / *printed*
1510		SCHLAGGENWALD (Slavkov) Haas & Czjizek 20th cent. / *printed*

1511		SCHLACKENWERTH (Ostrov) Pfeiffer & Löwenstein 20th cent. / *printed*
1512		LANGEWIESEN O. Schlegelmilch after 1892 / *printed*
1513		SCHLOTTENHOF Porzellanfabrik after 1893 / *printed*
1514	*Schoelcher*	PARIS, RUE DU FAUBOURG SAINT DENIS Soelcher 1800—1828 / *red*
1515	S^t.C. T	SAINT CLOUD H. & G. Trou 1722—1766 / *blue*
1516		ARZBERG C. Schumann after 1881 / *printed*
1517		SCHWARZENHAMMER Schumann & Schreider after 1905 / *printed*
1518		WEISSWASSER A. Schwaig after 1895 / *printed*

1519		KÖPPELSDORF-NORD Schoenau Bros, Swaine & Co. after 1854 / *printed*
1520	SCR	MILAN G. Richard 1874 / *printed*
1521		SELB Gräf & Krippner *c.* 1900 / *printed*
1522		SELB Gräf & Krippner *c.* 1900 / *printed*
1523	H&C? Selb	SELB Heinrich & Co. after 1896 / *printed*
1524		SELB Heinrich & Co. 1904 / *printed*
1525		SELB Heinrich & Co. 1911 / *printed*
1526		SELB Heinrich & Co. 1905 / *printed*
1527		SELB Heinrich & Co. 1914 / *printed*

1528

SELB
P. Müller
1928—1943 / *printed*

1529

SELB
L. Hutschenreuther
1858—1920 / *printed*

1530

SELB
P. Müller
1912—1924 / *printed*

1531

MITTERTEICH
J. Richter & Co.
20th cent. / *printed*

1532

SÈVRES
period of the Consulate
1803—1804 / *gold, various
colours*

1533

BOCK-WALLENDORF
Fasold & Stauch
after 1903 / *printed*

1534

FREIWALDAU (Gozdnica)
H. Schmidt
20th cent. / *blue*

1535

LONGTON
Shelley Potteries
1867 / *printed*

1536
1537

KÖNIGSZELT (Jaworzyna
Śląska)
Porzellanfabrik
after 1860 / *printed*

1538		TIEFENFURTH (Parowa) K. Steinmann G. m. b. H. after 1883 / *printed*
1539		SELB Krautheim & Adelberg G. m. b. H. after 1884 / *printed*
1540		SCHLAGGENWALD (Slavkov) Sommer & Matschak after 1904 / *printed*
1541		LANGEWIESEN O. Schlegelmilch after 1892 / *printed*
1542		SOPHIENTHAL Thomas & Co. after 1928 / *printed*
1543		SORAU (Żary) C. & E. Carstens after 1918 / *printed*
1544		SCHELTEN (Šelty) J. Palme after 1829 / *blue, impressed*
1545		SELB P. Müller after 1890 / *blue*
1546	 	SPECHTSBRUNN Porzellanfabrik after 1911 / *printed*

1547 1548	*Spode* SPODE	STOKE-ON-TRENT J. Spode *c.* 1790 / *printed*
1549	SPODE Stone China	STOKE-ON-TRENT J. Spode *c.* 1800 / *printed*
1550	Spode Felspar Porcelain	STOKE-ON-TRENT J. Spode 1800—1833 / *printed*
1551	Spode's Imperial	STOKE-ON-TRENT J. Spode 1800—1833 / *printed*
1552	SPODE SON & COPELAND	STOKE-ON-TRENT J. Spode *c.* 1833 / *printed*
1553	S+E	KRONACH Stockhardt & Schmidt-Eckert after 1912 / *printed*
1554	S.t C.	SAINT CLOUD P. Chicaneau *c.* 1677 / *blue*
1555	STONE coquerol et LEGROS PARIS	PARIS RUE SAINT MERRY Stone, Coquerel & Legros 1807—1849 / *blue*
1556 1557	StPM St. P. M.	STANOWITZ (Strzegom) C. Walter & Co. after 1873 / *blue*
1558	Staff's	FENTON Crown Staffordshire China after 1808 / *printed*

1559

STAFFORDSHIRE
FINE BONE CHINA
OF
ARTHUR BOWKER | FENTON
A. Bowker
19th cent. / *printed* |
| **1560** | | FENTON
Crown Staffordshire China
19th cent. / *printed* |
| **1561** |  | FENTON
Crown Staffordshire China
20th cent. / *printed* |
| **1562** |  | LONGTON
Royal Staffordshire China
after 1843 / *printed* |
| **1563** |  | LONGTON
T. Poole & Gladstone
after 1843 / *printed* |
| **1564** |

ROYAL
STANDARD
BONE CHINA
ENGLAND | LONGTON
Chapmans Ltd
after 1916 / *printed* |
| **1565**
1566 | | LONGTON
C. Amison & Co.
after 1875 / *printed*
c. 1900 / *printed* |

1567		TIEFENFURTH (Parowa) C. H. Tupack after 1802 / *printed*
1568		SAARGEMÜND Utzschneider & Co. after 1775 / *blue*
1569 **1570** **1571**		SUHL E. Schlegelmilch after 1861 / *blue*
1572 **1573**		LIMOGES Porcelaine de Casseaux 20th cent. / *printed*
1574		SCHWARZA-SAALBAHN E. & A. Müller after 1890 / *printed*
1575		KÖPPELSDORF-NORD Schoenau Bros, Swaine & Co. after 1854 / *printed*
1576	SWANSEA	SWANSEA L. W. Dillwyn 1814—1830 / *impressed*
1577	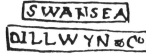	SWANSEA L. W. Dillwyn 1814—1830 / *blue*
1578		SWANSEA L. W. Dillwyn 1814—1870 / *blue*

1579		RUDOLSTADT L. Straus & Söhne after 1882 / *printed*
1580 **1581**	 	SCHWARZENHAMMER Schumann & Schreider after 1905 / *printed*
1582		SCEAUX De Bey, J. Chapelle 1763—1795 / *incised*
1583		LONGTON J. Shaw & Sons 20th cent. / *printed*
1584 **1585** **1586**		TETTAU G. C. Greiner after 1794 / *blue*
1587		TETTAU G. C. Greiner after 1794 / *blue*
1588		ZWICKAU C. Fischer after 1850 / *blue*
1589 **1590**		TANNAWA (Ždanov) F. J. Mayer 1840—1880 / *impressed*
1591		FRANKENTHAL Carl Theodor von der Pfalz 1762—1797 / *blue*

1592		FRANKENTHAL A. Bergdoll 1762—1775 / *blue*
1593 **1594**	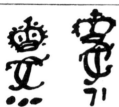	FRANKENTHAL Carl Theodor von der Pfalz 1770—1789 / *blue*
1595		VOLKSTEDT-RUDOLSTADT Porzellanfabrik 20th cent. / *printed*
1596		WALDENBURG (Walbrzych) C. Tielsch after 1895 / *printed*
1597		LUNÉVILLE P. L. Cyfflé; "Terre de Lorraine" end of 18th cent. / *blue*
1598		TETTAU Königliche Porzellanfabrik after 1885 / *printed*
1599		TETTAU Königliche Porzellanfabrik after 1885 / *printed*
1600		TETTAU Gerold & Co. after 1904 / *printed*

1601		TETTAU Gerold & Co. after 1904 / *printed*
1602		TETTAU Gerold & Co. after 1904 / *printed*
1603		LIMOGES C. Tharaud after 1919 / *printed*
1604		MARKTREDWITZ F. Thomas 1903—1908 / *printed*
1605		TILLOWITZ (Tulowice) R. Schlegelmilch after 1869 / *printed*
1606 1607 1608		KLÖSTERLE (Klášterec) Gräfliche Thun'sche Porzellanfabrik 1804—1830 / *blue, gold*
1609		KLÖSTERLE (Klášterec) Gräfliche Thun'sche Porzellanfabrik 1830—1893 / *impressed*
1610		KLÖSTERLE (Klášterec) Gräfliche Thun'sche Porzellanfabrik after 1893 / *printed*
1611		ZWICKAU C. Fischer after 1850 / *blue*

1612	*Tomaszów Mezer*	TOMASZÓW F. Mezer 1806 / *blue*
1613	☰ ✳ **TOMASZÓW** 1808	TOMASZÓW F. Mezer 1808 / *black*
1614	☰ ✳ **W TOMASZOWIE** 1808	TOMASZÓW F. Mezer 1808 / *black*
1615	*w Tomaszo*	TOMASZÓW F. Mezer 1806—1827 / *gold*
1616	*wie* *Tomaszów*	TOMASZÓW F. Mezer 1806—1827 / *gold*
1617		TETTAU Gerold & Co. after 1904 / *printed*
1618	**fTP.** **1812**	POTSCHAPPEL C. Thieme 1872 / *blue*
1619	**T.P.M.**	TIEFENFURTH (Parowa) P. Donath after 1883 / *blue*
1620	*Trentham* ROYAL CROWN POTTERY FINE BONE CHINA ENGLAND	LONGTON Trentham Bone China Ltd 20th cent. / *printed*

1621	F.F. Treviſo.1799	TREVISO Fontebasso Bros 1799 / *blue*
1622 1623	G.A.T.F G.A.F.F. Treviso Treviso.	TREVISO Fontebasso Bros beginning of 19th cent. / *blue*
1624		TRIPTIS Porzellanfabrik A. G. after 1891 / *printed*
1625	 W.T ENGLISH PORCELANY IR&Cº	COALPORT W. Taylor *c.* 1820 / *blue*
1626		POTSCHAPPEL C. Thieme after 1872 / *blue*
1627		UPPSALA Ekeby Aktiebolag from 1918 / *printed*
1628	U D	DALLWITZ (Dalovice) F. Urfus 1855—1875 / *impressed*
1629		UHLSTÄDT C. Alberti after 1837 / *printed*
1630	Ulm J	ULM J. J. Schmidt 1827—1833 / *blue*

1631		UNTERKÖDITZ Möller & Dippe after 1846 / *printed*
1632		SAINT UZE G. Revol Père & Fils after 1857 / *printed*
1633 **1634**		VENICE N. F. Hewelcke 1761—1763 / *incised, red*
1635		VINOVO Dr V. A. Gioanetti after 1780 / *blue*
1636		VINOVO Dr V. A. Gioanetti after 1780 / *incised*
1637		VENICE N. F. Hewelcke 1757—1765 / *red, gold*
1638		VISTA ALEGRE J. Ferreira Pinto Basto 1824—1840 / *blue*
1639 **1640**		VISTA ALEGRE J. Ferreira Pinto Basto after 1840 / *blue*
1641		BORDEAUX M. Vanier 1788—1790 / *blue, red, gold*
1642		SAINT VALLIER L. Boissonnet 20th cent. / *printed*

1643		VINOVO Dr V. A. Gioanetti *c.* 1800 / *blue*
1644		VENICE F. & G. Vezzi 1720—1727 / *blue*
1645		VENICE F. & G. Vezzi 1720—1727 / *blue*
1646		VENICE F. & G. Vezzi 1720—1727 / *red, blue, gold*
1647		VENICE F. & G. Vezzi 1720—1727 / *blue, incised*
1648		VENICE F. & G. Vezzi 1720—1727 / *red, blue, green*
1649		ILMENAU Greiner and successors 20th cent. / *printed*
1650		VENICE F. & G. Vezzi 1720—1727 / *blue*
1651 **1652**		LAVENO Società Ceramica Italiana 20th. cent. / *printed*
1653 **1654**		KLOSTER VESSRA Porzellanfabrik 1892 / *printed*

1655	*V.F*	VINOVO Fornari 19th cent. / *blue*
1656 **1657**		ALT-ROHLAU (Stará Role) Porzellanfabrik Victoria A. G. after 1883 / *printed*
1658		HOF MOSCHENDORF O. Reinecke after 1878 / *printed*
1659		LONGTON Cartwright & Edwards Ltd after 1851 / *printed*
1660		SHELTON J. & W. Ridgeway 1850—1858 / *printed*
1661 **1662**		COBRIDGE Viking Pottery Co. 1936 / *printed*
1663	*villers Cottereti*	CHANTILLY Villers Cotterets 1770—1785 / *blue*
1664		SCHORNDORF Bauer & Pfeiffer 1904 / *printed*

1665	*Porcelana de 1850 Vista Alegre em Portugal*	VISTA ALEGRE J. Ferreira Pinto Basto 1850 / *blue*
1666	Vista Alegre Est. 1824	VISTA ALEGRE J. Ferreira Pinto Basto 20th cent. / *printed*
1667 **1668**		VOHENSTRAUSS J. Seltmann after 1901 / *printed*
1669		VOLKSTEDT-RUDOLSTADT K. Ens after 1898 / *printed*
1670	BAVARIA *Johann Seltmann Vohenstrauß*	VOHENSTRAUSS J. Seltmann 20th cent. / *printed*
1671	*Volokitine miKlachefsky*	VOLOKITINO A. Miklaszewski 19th cent. / *red*
1672		CHODAU (Chodov) Porges von Portheim after 1845 / *impressed*
1673		VOLKSTEDT-RUDOLSTADT R. Eckert & Co. after 1895 / *printed*

1674	FRANKENTHAL J. N. van Recum 1797—1799 / *blue*
1675	BERLIN W. C. Wegely 1751—1757 / *blue, impressed,* *incised*
1676	BERLIN W. C. Wegely 1751—1757 / *blue, impressed*
1677 **1678**	WÜRZBURG C. Geyger 1775—1780 / *impressed*
1679 **1680**	BORDEAUX P. & J. Verneuilh 1781—1787 / *blue, gold, red*
1681 **1682** **1683**	WORCESTER Dr J. Wall 1751—1783 / *blue*
1684	LONGTON HALL W. Littler 1753—1760 / *blue*
1685	LOWESTOFT imitations of Worcester porcelain end of 18th cent. / *blue*
1686 **1687**	WALLENDORF J. W. Hamann and G. and J. Greiner 1764—1800 / *blue*
1688	WALLENDORF J. W. Hamann 1764—1778 / *blue*
1689	WEISSWASSER A. Schweig after 1895 / *printed*

1690	VISCHE L. Birago 1766—1768 / *impressed*
1691	HORN H. Wehinger & Co. 1905 / *impressed*
1692	WALLENDORF H. Schaubach after 1926 / *printed*
1693	WISTRITZ (Bystřice) Krantzberger, Mayer & Purkert after 1911 / *printed*
1694	LIPPELSDORF Wagner & Apel after 1877 / *printed*
1695	TURN (Trnovany) E. Wahliss before 1918 / *printed*
1696	MARKTREDWITZ F. Neukirchner after 1916 / *printed*
1697	WALDERSHOF Porzellanfabrik 1907—1924 / *printed*

1698		WALDSASSEN Bareuther after 1866 / *printed*
1699		WEINGARTEN R. Wohlfinger after 1882 / *printed*
1700 **1701**		WEIDEN Bauscher Bros after 1881 / *printed*
1702		BLANKENHAIN C. & A. Carstens after 1790 / *printed*
1703		BLANKENHAIN C. & A. Carstens after 1790 / *printed*
1704		WEISSENSTADT Dürbeck & Rückdäschel after 1920 / *printed*
1705		WEISSWASSER A. Schweig after 1895 / *printed*
1706		OESLAU W. Goebel after 1879 / *printed*
1707		ELGERSBURG E. & F. C. Arnoldi after 1808 / *blue*

1708		WALDERSHOF J. Haviland after 1907 / *printed*
1709		VIENNA, AUGARTEN Porzellanfabrik after 1922 / *blue*
1710		WILHELMSBURG Porzellanfabrik after 1882 / *printed*
1711		WEIDEN C. Seltmann after 1911 / *printed*
1712	MANUFACTURE À.WOLOKITIN: G d Tchernigow A.D'Miklachefsky	VOLOKITINO A. Miklaszewski 19th cent. / *red*
1713	 *Worcester*	WORCESTER R. Holdship 1751 / *printed*
1714	PW	WEINGARTEN R. Wohlfinger after 1882 / *printed*
1715		SCHORNDORF Porzellanmanufaktur 1904—1939 / *printed*
1716		LUDWIGSBURG Wilhelmus Rex 1816—1824 / *red, gold*
1717 **1718**		LONGTON HALL W. Littler 1751—1753 / *blue*

1719 1720 1721		ZÜRICH S. Gessner & A. Spengler 1763—1790 / *blue*
1722		ZELL-HARMERSBACH G. Schmider 1820—1840 / *printed*
1723		REHAU Zeh, Scherzer & Co. 1880—1930 / *printed*
1724		REHAU Zeh, Scherzer & Co. after 1880 / *printed*
1725		REHAU Zeh, Scherzer & Co. after 1880 / *printed*
1726		ZELL-HARMERSBACH J. F. Lenz 1846—1867 / *printed*
1727 1728		ZELL-HARMERSBACH G. Schmider 19th cent. / *printed*
1729		ZELL-HARMERSBACH G. Schmider 19th cent. / *printed*

1730	ZELL	ZELL-HARMERSBACH J. F. Lenz 1846—1867 / *printed*
1731		OBERHOHNDORF F. Kaestner after 1883 / printed
1732	J Z & Co	SELB J. Zeidler & Co. after 1866 / *impressed*
1733		SEEDORF Müller & Co. 1907 / *printed*
1734		ALT-ROHLAU (Stará Role) M. Zdekauer 1918—1938 / *printed*
1735		ZWEIBRÜCKEN, GUTENBRUNN Christian IV of Pfalz- Zweibrücken 1767—1775 / *blue*
1736		REHAU Zeh, Scherzer & Co. *c.* 1880 / *printed*
1737		BUDAPEST Zsolnay after 1862 / *printed*

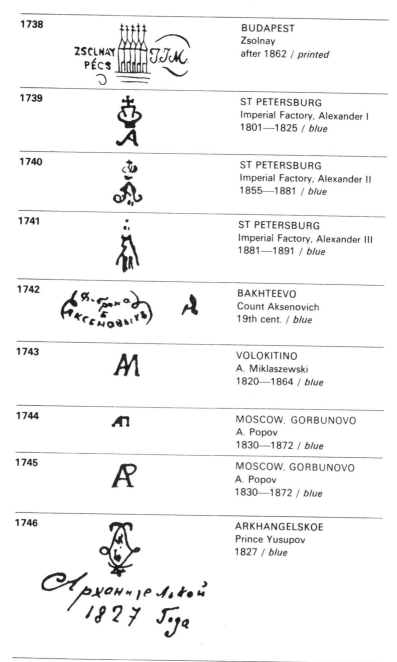

1738	**BUDAPEST** Zsolnay after 1862 / *printed*
1739	**ST PETERSBURG** Imperial Factory, Alexander I 1801—1825 / *blue*
1740	**ST PETERSBURG** Imperial Factory, Alexander II 1855—1881 / *blue*
1741	**ST PETERSBURG** Imperial Factory, Alexander III 1881—1891 / *blue*
1742	**BAKHTEEVO** Count Aksenovich 19th cent. / *blue*
1743	**VOLOKITINO** A. Miklaszewski 1820—1864 / *blue*
1744	**MOSCOW, GORBUNOVO** A. Popov 1830—1872 / *blue*
1745	**MOSCOW, GORBUNOVO** A. Popov 1830—1872 / *blue*
1746	**ARKHANGELSKOE** Prince Yusupov 1827 / *blue*
1747	**ARKHANGELSKOE** Prince Yusupov 1831 / *blue*

1748		BARANOVKA F. Mezer 1828 / *blue*
1749		BARANOVKA F. Mezer 1826 / *blue*
1750		ST PETERSBURG S. Batenin 1812—1832 / *blue*
1751		BARANOVKA M. Gripari after 1895 / *impressed*
1752		FRYAZINO Barmin Bros 1810—1850 / *blue*
1753	Бар минь хъ	FRYAZINO Barmin Bros 1810—1850 / *printed*
1754		FRYAZINO Barmin Bros 1810—1850 / *printed*
1755	САФРОНОВА С	MOSCOW, NAROTKAYA Safronov 1830—1840 / *blue*
1756	СЗКБ ф	ST PETERSBURG S. Batenin 1812—1832 / *blue*

1757 	BUDY M. S. Kuznetsov 1887 / *blue, printed*
1758	NOVOKHARITINO T. I. Kuznetsov after 1800 / *blue*
1759 **1760** 	ST PETERSBURG Imperial Factory, Catherine the Great 1762—1796 / *blue*
1761	ST PETERSBURG Catherine the Great, court porcelain 1762—1796 / *blue*
1762 ФГ ГУЛИНА	MOSCOW, RYAZAN J. Gulyn 1830—1850 / *blue*
1763 	VERBILKI F. Gardner after 1787 / *blue*
1764 **1765**	VERBILKI F. Gardner after 1787 / *blue*
1766 ГАРДНЕРZ	VERBILKI F. Gardner after 1787 / *blue, impressed*

1767		VERBILKI
1768	Г ꟙ	F. Gardner
		after 1787 / *blue, impressed*

1769		GORODNITZA (Horodnica)
		W. Rulikowski
		1856—1880 / *red*

1770		GORODNITZA (Horodnica)
		W. Rulikowski
		1856—1880 / *red*

1771		GORODNITZA (Horodnica)
		W. Rulikowski
		1856—1880 / *red*

1772		GORODNITZA (Horodnica)
		W. Rulikowski
		1856—1880 / *red*

1773	ГИНТЕЬР ᵛКо	MOSCOW
		T. Gunther & Co.
		1818—1876 / *printed*

1774		KORZEC
		F. Mezer
		beginning of 19th cent. / *red*

1775		KORZEC
		F. Mezer
		beginning of 19th cent. / *red*

1776		ST PETERSBURG
		S. V. Kornilov
		1835—1885 / *printed*

1777 **1778**		NOVOKHARITINO Kuznetsov Bros beginning of 19th cent. / *printed*
1779		DULEVO S. T. Kuznetsov 1832 — 2nd half of 19th cent. *printed*
1780		DULEVO S. T. Kuznetsov after 1889 / *printed*
1781 **1782**		DULEVO S. T. Kuznetsov 1832 — 2nd half of 19th cent. *printed*
1783		RIGA M. S. Kuznetsov 1842 / *printed*
1784		RIGA M. S. Kuznetsov 2nd half of 19th cent. / *printed*
1785		RIGA M. S. Kuznetsov beginning of 20th cent. / *printed*
1786 **1787**		VOLKHOV I. E. Kuznetsov 1878 / *printed*
1788		BUDY M. S. Kuznetsov 1882 / *printed*

1789	ФАБРИКИ М.С.КУЗНЕЦОВА ТВЕР ГУБЕР.	TVER M. S. Kuznetsov 1891 / printed
1790	С.Г.К. МОРЬЕ П. I.	MORE C. Golenichev-Kutuzov 1847—1887 / blue
1791		ST PETERSBURG Imperial Factory, Nicholas II 1891—1917 / blue
1792	АІ АІ	MOSCOW, SPASSK D. Nasonov 1811—1813 / blue
1793	БРАТЬЕВЬ НОВЫХЬ	MOSCOW Novoi Bros 1820—1840 / printed
1794	П.	ST PETERSBURG Imperial Factory, Paul I 1796—1801 / blue
1795	П П:К.	ST PETERSBURG Paul I, court tableware 1796—1801 / blue
1796		MOSCOW, GORBUNOVO A. Popov after 1872 / blue
1797	ПОПОВЫ	MOSCOW, GORBUNOVO A. Popov 1800—1872 / blue

1798	VOLOKITINO A. Miklaszewski 1820—1826 / *blue*
1799 HX	KUSYAEV N. Khrapunov 1820—1840 / *blue*
1800	ST PETERSBURG (Leningrad) M. V. Lomonosov Factory 1917 / *blue*
1801	ST PETERSBURG (Leningrad) M. V. Lomonosov Factory 1917 / *blue*
1802	**CHINESE PORCELAIN** **A. Reign marks (nien hao)** produced during the Hung Wu period 1368—1399 / *blue*
1803 	Hung Wu 1368—1399 / *blue*
1804	produced during the Yung Lo period 1403—1425 / *blue*

1805

Yung Lo
1403—1425 / *blue*

1806

produced during the Yung Lo period
1403—1425 / *printed*

1807

大明宣
德年製

produced during the Hsüan Tê period under the great Ming dynasty
1426—1436 / *blue*

1808

宣德

Hsüan Tê
1426—1436 / *blue*

1809

produced during the Hsüan Tê period under the great Ming dynasty
1426—1436 / *printed*

1810 化 大 年 明 製 成	produced during the Ch'êng Hua period under the great Ming dynasty 1465—1488 / *blue*
1811 成 化	Ch'êng Hua 1465—1488 / *blue*
1812 年 成 製 化	produced during the Ch'êng Hua period 1465—1488 / *blue*
1813	produced during the Ch'êng Hua period 1465—1488 / *printed*
1814 治 大 年 明 製 弘	produced during the Hung Chih period under the great Ming dynasty 1488—1505 / *blue*
1815 弘 治	Hung Chih 1488—1505 / *blue*

1816	德年製 大明正	produced during the Chêng Tê period under the great Ming dynasty 1506—1522 / *blue*
1817	正 德	Chêng Tê 1506—1522 / *blue*
1818	靖年製 大明嘉	produced during the Chia Ch'ing period under the great Ming dynasty 1522—1567 / *blue*
1819	嘉 靖	Chia Ch'ing 1522—1567 / *blue*
1820	慶年製 大明隆	produced during the Lung Ch'ing period under the great Ming dynasty 1567—1573 / *blue*

1821

Lung Ch'ing
1567—1573 / *blue*

1822

produced during the Wan Li period under the great Ming dynasty
1573—1620 / *blue*

1823

Wan Li
1573—1620 / *blue*

1824

produced during the T'ien Ch'i period under the great Ming dynasty
1621—1628 / *blue*

1825

produced during the Ch'ung Chên period
1628—1643 / *blue*

| 1826 | 治 年 製 | 大 清 順 | produced during the Shun Chih period under the great Ch'ing dynasty
1644—1622 / *blue* |

| 1827 | 順 治 | Shun Chih
1644—1662 / *blue* |

| 1828 | | produced during the Shun Chih period under the great Ch'ing dynasty
1644—1662 / *printed* |

| 1829 | | Shun Chih
1644—1662 / *calligraphic* |

| 1830 | 熙 年 製 | 大 清 康 | produced during the K'ang Hsi period under the great Ch'ing dynasty
1662—1723 / *blue* |

| 1831 | 康 熙 | K'ang Hsi
1662—1723 / *blue* |

1832		produced during the K'ang Hsi period under the great Ch'ing dynasty 1662—1723 / *printed*
1833		K'ang Hsi 1662—1723 / *calligraphic*
1834		produced during the Yung Chêng period under the great Ch'ing dynasty 1723—1736 / *blue*
1835		Yung Chêng 1723—1736 / *blue*
1836		produced during the Yung Chêng period under the great Ch'ing dynasty 1723—1736 / *printed*
1837		Yung Chêng 1723—1736 / *calligraphic*

1838

大清乾隆年製

produced during the Ch'ien Lung period under the great Ch'ing dynasty
1736—1796 / *blue*

1839

乾隆

Ch'ien Lung
1736—1796 / *blue*

1840

produced during the Ch'ien Lung period under the great Ch'ing dynasty
1736—1796 / *printed*

1841

Ch'ien Lung
1736—1796 / *calligraphic*

1842

嘉慶年製

produced during the Chia Ch'ing period
1796—1821 / *blue*

1843

嘉慶

Chia Ch'ing
1796—1821 / *blue*

1844

produced during the Chia Ch'ing period under the great Ch'ing dynasty
1796—1821 / *printed*

1845

Chia Ch'ing
1796—1821 / *calligraphic*

1846

produced during the Tao Kuang period under the great Ch'ing dynasty
1821—1851 / *blue*

1847

Tao Kuang
1821—1851 / blue

1848

produced during the Tao Kuang period under the great Ch'ing dynasty
1821—1851 / *printed*

1849

Tao Kuang
1821—1851 / *calligraphic*

| 1850 | 豐年製 大清咸 | produced during the Hsien Fêng period under the great Ch'ing dynasty
1851—1862 / *blue* |

| 1851 | | Hsien Fêng
1851—1862 / *blue* |

| 1852 | | produced during the Hsien Fêng period under the great Ch'ing dynasty
1851—1862 / *printed* |

| 1853 | | Hsien Fêng
1851—1862 / *calligraphic* |

| 1854 | 治年製 大清同 | produced during the T'ung Chih period under the great Ch'ing dynasty
1862—1875 / *blue* |

| 1855 | 同治 | T'ung Chih
1862—1875 |

1856

produced during the T'ung Chih period under the great Ch'ing dynasty
1862—1875 / *printed*

1857

T'ung Chih
1862—1875 / *calligraphic*

1858

produced during the Kuang Hsü period under the great Ch'ing dynasty
1875—1908 / *blue*

1859

Kuang Hsü
1875—1908 / *blue*

1860

produced during the Kuang Hsü period under the great Ch'ing dynasty
1875—1908 / *printed*

1861

Kuang Hsü
1875—1908 / *calligraphic*

1862	奇石寶	閟之珍	B. Hall Marks Gem among precious wares made of precious stones
1863	奇玉宝	閟之珍	Gem among precious wares made of jade
1864	景濂堂	倣古製	produced according to ancient models in Ching-lien Hall
1865	益右	堂製	produced in the I-yu Hall
1866	仁和館.		Jên-ho-kuan after the year 1000 Sung dynasty
1867	樞府		Shu-fu 2nd half of 13th cent. Yuan dynasty

1868

佳器 玉堂

Beautiful vessel from the Jade Hall
after 1606
Ming dynasty

1869

德馨堂製

produced in the Tê-hsing Hall
1573—1620

1870

福藩製造

produced in Fu-kien
Ming dynasty

1871

慎德堂製

produced in the Ch'ên-tê Hall
1573—1620

1872

芷蘭齋製

produced in the Chih-lan Pavilion
17th cent.

1873

聚順美玉堂製

produced in the Hall of Beautiful Jade in Chü-shun
end of 17th cent.

1874	堂製 林玉	produced in the Lin-yü Hall 1662—1722
1875	堂製 玉海	produced in the Yü-hai Hall beginning of 18th cent.
1876	堂製 攻寸	produced in the Yu-yü Hall beginning of 18th cent.
1877	堂製 奇玉	produced in the Hall of Precious Jade beginning of 18th cent.
1878		produced in the Yü-hai Hall 1662—1722
1879	堂製 養和	produced in the Yang-ho Hall 1723—1735

1880		produced in the Tan-ning-chai Pavilion 1736—1795
1881	故是堂製	produced in the Ching-wei Hall 1736—1795
1882	彩潤堂製	produced in the T'sai-jun Hall 1723—1735
1883		produced in the T'sai-hsiu Hall 1821—1850
1884	大樹堂製	produced in the Hall of Big Trees 1821—1850
1885	慎德堂博古製	produced in the ancient manner in the Shên-tê Hall 1820—1850

1886	崇 猗 堂	The Lü-i Hall 18th—19th cent.
1887	齋 雅 大	The Ta Ya Ch'ai Pavilion *c.* 1900
1888	張 家 造	**C. Artists´ marks** made by Chang-chia after 1600
1889	道 壺 人 隱	the Taoist Hu-yin *c.* 1600
1890	魟 眠	Wang Shou-ming after 1600
1891	國 建 年 中 製 靖	produced in the first year of the new establishment of the country 1573

1892		made by Chin-shih in the *i chou* year, during the T'ien Ch'i reign 1597
1893		modelled by Ch'en Wen in the *ting yu* year, during the Wan Li reign 17th cent.
1894		Ch'en-te the Hermit 17th cent.
1895		Shang-su 1735—1795
1896		Chung family 13th cent.
1897		Ch'en-kuo 1662—1722

1898		made by Yüan Hsin-hsing 19th cent.
1899		made by Kung Yüan-chi c. 1700
1900		made by Ch'en T'ien-sui 1662—1722
1901		made by Sheng-kao in the last day of the fourth month of the third year of the Chia Ch'ing reign 1798
1902		Pai-shih c. 1724

1903 made by Chiang Ming-hao
1662—1722

1904 Chao-ch'in
beginning of 18th cent.

1905 Lai
1662—1722

1906  made by Liang-chi in the *wu chen* year
1808

1907  made by Chiang Ming-hao
beginning of 18th cent.

1908  made by Li Chên-fa
beginning of 19th cent.

1909 made by Wang Tso-t'ing
c. 1800

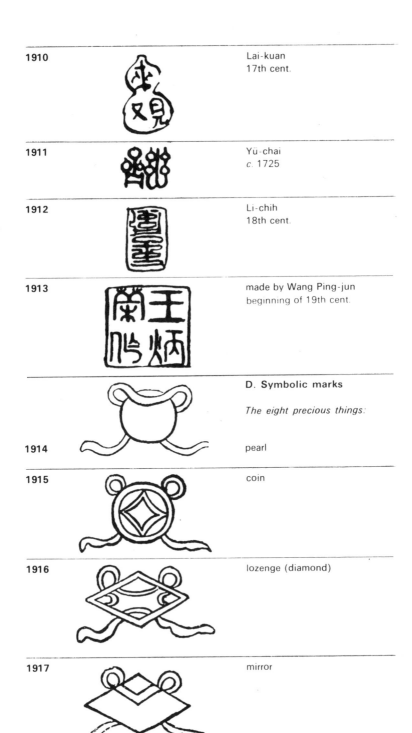

1910	Lai-kuan 17th cent.
1911	Yü-chai *c.* 1725
1912	Li-chih 18th cent.
1913	made by Wang Ping-jun beginning of 19th cent.

D. Symbolic marks

The eight precious things:

1914	pearl
1915	coin
1916	lozenge (diamond)
1917	mirror

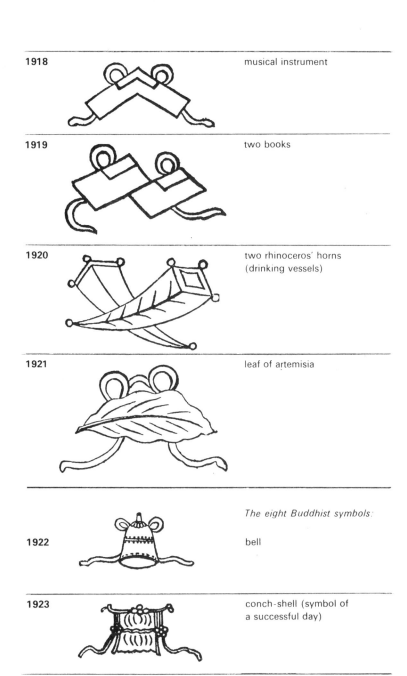

1918		musical instrument
1919		two books
1920		two rhinoceros' horns (drinking vessels)
1921		leaf of artemisia
		The eight Buddhist symbols:
1922		bell
1923		conch-shell (symbol of a successful day)
1924		umbrella

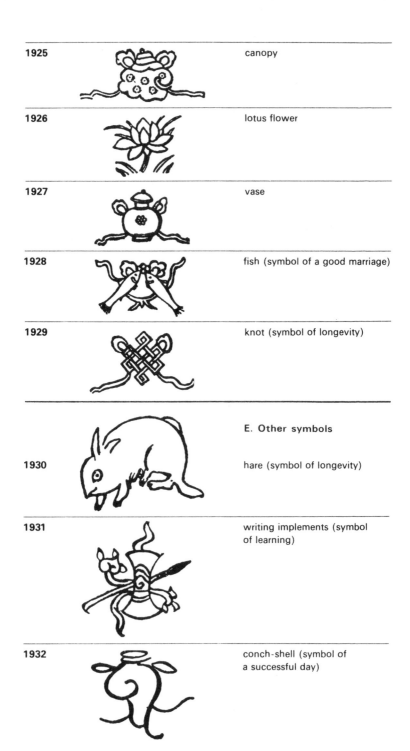

1925	canopy
1926	lotus flower
1927	vase
1928	fish (symbol of a good marriage)
1929	knot (symbol of longevity)

E. Other symbols

1930	hare (symbol of longevity)
1931	writing implements (symbol of learning)
1932	conch-shell (symbol of a successful day)

1933  leaf

1934  leaf (a different form)

1935  mushroom

1936  mushroom (a different form)

1937 peach and bat (symbol of happiness)

1938  musical instrument

1939

eight-petalled flower

1940

five-petalled flower

1941

bud

1942

four-petalled flower

JAPANESE PORCELAIN

1943

吳　五
祥　良
瑞　大
造　甫

ARITA (Hizen prov.)
Gorodayu Go Shonzui
after 1510

1944

五　倣
良　余
大　祖
甫　先
所　祥
製　瑞

ARITA (Hizen prov.)
Shonzui Gorodayu (imitation)
19th cent.

1945

ARITA (Hizen prov.)
Inscription: wealth, honour
and everlasting spring
19th cent.

1946

ARITA (Hizen prov.)
Inscription: gem of our
precious wares
19th cent.

1947

ARITA (Hizen prov.)
Ya (elegance)
19th cent.

1948

ARITA (Hizen prov.)
Ho (costliness)
19th cent.

1949

ARITA (Hizen prov.)
Fu ku (happiness)
19th cent.

1950

ARITA (Hizen prov.)
Kin (gold)
19th cent.

1951

ARITA (Hizen prov.)
Ka (prosperity)
19th cent.

1952		ARITA (Hizen prov.) unknown mark 18th cent.
1953		ARITA (Hizen prov.) unknown mark (a Chinese character) 18th century
1954		ARITA (Hizen prov.) Arita (name of city and port) 18th cent.
1955		ARITA (Hizen prov.) Zoshutei sampo (Sampo) 19th cent.
1956		ARITA (Hizen prov.) Hichozan Shimpo 19th cent.
1957		ARITA (Hizen prov.) Fukagawa 19th cent.

1958	三川内 平戸製	HIRADO (Hizen prov.) Mikahawacha (factory) 19th cent.
1959	制衣 平戸	HIRADO (Hizen prov.) produced in Hirado 19th cent.
1960		NABESHIMA (Hizen prov.) imitation of old porcelain from Nabeshima 19th cent.
1961	亀山製	KAMEYAMA (Hizen prov.) produced in Kameyama lst half of 19th cent.
1962	珎玩 道食	KUTANI (Kaga prov.) Dosuku (costliness) 18th cent.
1963	九谷	KUTANI (Kaga prov.) place mark 19th cent.
1964	福	KUTANI (Kaga prov.) Fu ku (happiness) 19th cent.
1965	福	KUTANI (Kaga prov.) Fu ku (happiness) 19th cent.

1966

KUTANI (Kaga prov.)
Sei (produced in Kutani)
19th cent.

1967

KUTANI (Kaga prov.)
city arms
19th cent.

1968

KUTANI (Kaga prov.)
Fu ku (happiness)
19th cent.

1969

KUTANI (Kaga prov.)
Fu ku (happiness)
19th cent.

1970

九谷造　大日本

KUTANI (Kaga prov.)
produced in Kutani, in Great
Japan
19th cent.

1971

KUTANI (Kaga prov.)
Tozan (mark representing
the clay used)
19th cent.

1972

KUTANI (Kaga prov.)
Ohi (factory mark)
19th cent.

1973

KUTANI (Kaga prov.)
Shiozo (potter)
19th cent.

1974

KUTANI (Kaga prov.)
Fu ku (happiness)
20th cent.

1975

KUTANI (Kaga prov.)
Tozan (mark representing
the clay used)
19th cent.

1976	大日本九谷製 久錦画製 [seal]	KUTANI (Kaga prov.) produced by Yeiraku in Kutani 19th cent.
1977	永樂造 発九谷	KUTANI (Kaga prov.) produced by Kioruku in Great Japan 19th cent.
1978	九谷造 大日本	KUTANI (Kaga prov.) produced in Kutani, in Great Japan 19th cent.
1979	綿野製 景德園	KUTANI (Kaga prov.) Kichii Watano 20th cent.
1980	姫路製	HIMEJI (Harima prov.) produced in Himeji *c.* 1826

1981	東山 播陽	HIMEJI (Harima prov.) produced from Tozan clay 20th cent.
1982	榎本叟	SAKURAI (Setsu prov.) place mark 19th. cent.
1983	吉向	OSAKA (Setsu prov.) Kichiko (potter) 19th cent.
1984	可樂	KOBE (Setsu prov.) place mark 19th cent.
1985	京都	KYOTO (Yamashiro prov.) place mark 19th cent.
1986		KYOTO (Yamashiro prov.) Rokubei (potter) beginning of 19th cent.

1987		YEIRAKU (Yamashiro prov.) produced in Yeiraku beginning of 19th cent.
1988		YEIRAKU (Yamashiro prov.) place mark 19th cent.
1989		YEIRAKU (Yamashiro prov.) place mark 19th cent.
1990		YEIRAKU (Yamashiro prov.) place mark 19th cent.
1991		RANTEI (Yamashiro prov.) pure jewel from Rantei 19th cent.
1992		RANTEI (Yamashiro prov.) place name 19th cent.

1993	亀岳 書こ之	KYOTO (Yamashiro prov.) produced by Kisui end of 19th cent.
1994	偕樂 園製	KYOTO (Yamashiro prov.) produced by Kisui end of 19th cent.
1995	三樂 園製	KYOTO (Yamashiro prov.) produced by Kisui end of 19th cent.
1996	扎園造	KYOTO (Yamashiro prov.) produced by Kiyen 19th cent.
1997	大日本 香齋製	KYOTO (Yamashiro prov.) produced by Kosai *c.* 1856
1998	香齋園	KYOTO (Yamashiro prov.) produced by Kosai *c.* 1850
1999	大日本 清風造	KYOTO (Yamashiro prov.) produced by Seifu 19th cent.

2000

情風 (seal mark)

KYOTO (Yamashiro prov.)
produced by Seifu
19th cent.

2001

周平　民形

KYOTO (Yamashiro prov.)
Ogari Shuhei (potter)
c. 1800

2002

褧之　左平

KYOTO (Yamashiro prov.)
produced by Sahei
19th cent.

2003

清製　幹山

KYOTO (Yamashiro prov.)
carefully produced by Kanzan
19th cent.

2004

KYOTO (Yamashiro prov.)
Kenzan (potter)
19th cent. / *brown*

2005

香山造　眞葛窯

KYOTO
(Yamashiro prov.)
Makuzu Kozan (potter)
2nd half of 19th cent.

2006

玉清製　復春軒

KYOTO (Yamashiro prov.)
produced in Gyokusei
2nd half of 19th cent.

2007	嘉永元年 南紀男山製	OTOKOYAMA (Kii prov.) produced in Otokoyama 1848
2008	湖東	KOTO (Omi prov.) place mark 1830—1860
2009	鳴鳳	KOTO (Omi prov.) Meiho (potter) 19th cent.
2010	尾張	OVARI (Ovari prov.) place mark 19th cent.
2011	瀬戸	SETO (Ovari prov.) place mark 19th cent.
2012	大日本 瀬戸製	SETO (Ovari prov.) produced in Seto in Great Japan 19th cent.

2013

加藤勘四郎

SETO (Ovari prov.)
Kato Kanshiro (family of
potters)
19th cent.

2014

川本
枡吉

SETO (Ovari prov.)
Kawamoto Masakichi
(family of potters)
19th. cent.

2015

大日本
羊介製

SETO (Ovari prov.)
produced by Hansuke in Great
Japan
19th cent.

2016

SETO (Ovari prov.)
tortoise as the mark of local
porcelain
19th —20th cent.

2017 	NAGOYA (Ovari prov.) Kaisha (company producing enamel porcelain) 20th cent.
2018	NAGOYA (Ovari prov.) place mark 19th cent.
2019 陶 玉 園 製	TOGYOKU (Mino prov.) produced in Togyoku 19th cent.
2020 日 本 美 濃 國 加 藤 五 輔 製	TOGYOKU (Mino prov.) produced by Kato Gosuke in Mino prov. 19th cent.

2021	SAMPEI (Awaji prov.) Kashu Sampei (place mark) end of 19th cent.
2022	SATSUMA (Satsuma prov.) Hoju (potter) 1780—1800
2023 	SATSUMA (Satsuma prov.) Hohei (potter) 1820—1840
2024	SATSUMA (Satsuma prov.) Seikozan (potter) 1830
2025	SATSUMA (Satsuma prov.) place mark 19th cent.
2026	SATSUMA (Satsuma prov.) Hoyu (potter) *c.* 1840
2027	SATSUMA (Satsuma prov.) Hoko or Yoshimitzu 1860

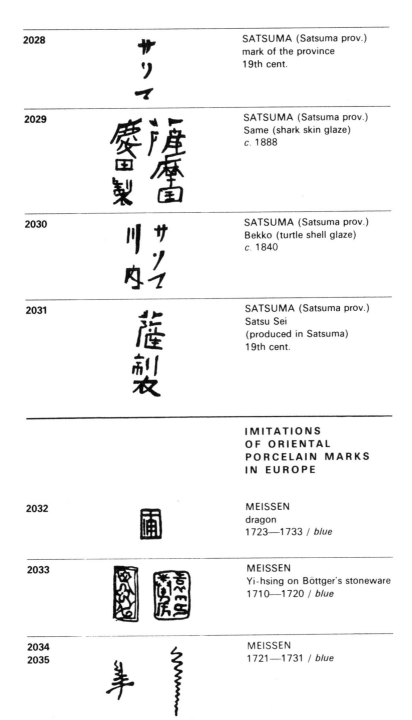

2028		SATSUMA (Satsuma prov.) mark of the province 19th cent.
2029		SATSUMA (Satsuma prov.) Same (shark skin glaze) *c.* 1888
2030		SATSUMA (Satsuma prov.) Bekko (turtle shell glaze) *c.* 1840
2031		SATSUMA (Satsuma prov.) Satsu Sei (produced in Satsuma) 19th cent.

IMITATIONS
OF ORIENTAL
PORCELAIN MARKS
IN EUROPE

2032		MEISSEN dragon 1723—1733 / *blue*
2033		MEISSEN Yi-hsing on Böttger's stoneware 1710—1720 / *blue*
2034 2035		MEISSEN 1721—1731 / *blue*

2036 2037		MEISSEN dragon 1723—1733 / *blue*
2038 2039		MEISSEN caduceus 1721—1722 / *blue*
2040 2041		BOW T. Frye 1755—1760 / *blue*
2042 2043		DERBY W. Duesbury 1770—1800 / *blue*
2044		DERBY W. Duesbury 1770—1800 / *blue*
2045		CHELSEA N. Sprimont & C. Gouyn 1745—1750 / *blue*
2046		CAUGHLEY T. Turner ("dressed number") 1783—1799 / *blue*
2047 2048 2049		CAUGHLEY T. Turner 1783—1799 / *blue*

2050 **2051**		CAUGHLEY T. Turner 1783—1799 / *blue*
2052		CAUGHLEY T. Turner 1783—1799 / *blue, red*
2053		WORCESTER 1755—1790 / *blue, red*
2054		PLYMOUTH W. Cookworthy 1768—1770 / *blue, red,* *incised in gold*
2055		STOKE-ON-TRENT T. Minton from 1821 / *blue*
2056		RÖRSTRAND Haancho after 1884 / *printed*
2057		MITTERTEICH J. Riber & Co. after 1888 / *printed*
2058		ANSBACH Markgräfliche Porzellanmanu- faktur 1757—1790 / *blue*
2059		VOLKSTEDT-RUDOLSTADT R. Eckert & Co. after 1895 / *printed*

2060

TURN (Trnovany)
Riessner & Kessel
after 1892 / *printed*

2061

ALT-ROHLAU (Stará Role)
Porzellanfabrik Viktoria A. G.
after 1883 / *printed*

BIBLIOGRAPHY

J. F. Blacker, Chats on Oriental China, *London 1908*

M. Brunet, Les marques de Sèvres, *Paris 1953*

W. Burton, and *R. L. Hobson*, Handbook of Marks on Pottery and Porcelain, *London 1909*

W. Chaffers, Collector's Handbook of Marks and Monograms on Pottery and Porcelain, *3rd edition, London 1952*

L. Chroscicki, Porcelana — znaki wytwórni europejskich, *Warsaw 1974*

J. P. Cushion and *W. B. Honey*, Handbook of Pottery and Porcelain Marks, *London 1956*

L. Danckert, Handbuch des europäischen Porzellans, *Munich 1957*

Geoffrey A. Godden, Encyclopaedia of British Pottery and Porcelain Marks, *London 1964*

J. G. Graesse and *E. Jaennicke*, Vollständiges Verzeichnis der auf älterem und neuem Porzellan, Steingut usw. befindlichen Marken. Letzte Neubearbeitung von A. und L. Behse, *22nd edition, Brunswick 1967*

H. Jedding, Europäisches Porzellan, *vol. 1, Munich 1971*

R. M. Kovel and *H. Terry*, Dictionary of Marks. Pottery and Porcelain, *New York 1953*

G. Lukomsky, Russisches Porzellan 1744—1923, *Berlin 1924*

M. Penkala, European Porcelain. A Handbook for the Collector, *London 1947*

E. Poche, Böhmisches Porzellan, *Prague 1956*

R. Rückert, Meissner Porzellan 1710—1810. Katalog der Ausstellung, *Munich 1966*

A. Schönberger, Deutsches Porzellan, *Munich 1949*

M. Swinarski and *L. Chroscicki*, Znaki Porcelany Europejskiej i Polskiej Ceramiki, *Poznań 1949*

C. Jordan Thorn, Handbook of Old Pottery and Porcelain Marks, *New York 1947*

INDEX OF MANUFACTURERS / ARTISTS

Adderley Watership 388 —390
Advenir & Lamare 387
Ahrenfeld, C. 565, 566
Aigmont, d' — Desmares 567,568
Aksenovich, count 1742
Albert, R. 564
Alberti, C. 1629
"Alexandra Porcelain-Works"
   154, 157
Alexander I 1739
Alexander II 1740
Alexander III 1741
Allen, R. 398 —400, 1187
Alluaud, J. F. 1124
Alton China 402
Amison, C. & Co. 1565, 1566
"Amphora" 6
Anchor period 275 —7
Anger, A. C. 457
Antonibon, E. P. 26, 27
Antonibon family 535, 1279,
   1280, 1302 —4, 1308
Antonibon, G. B. 854, 1307
Aponte, de, Pickmann & Co. 1356,
   1357, 1389
"Arabia" 145, 158, 443 —6, 931,
   932, 1333
Aranda, count — Cloostermans, P.
   360 —2
Arnoldi, E. & F. C. 384, 774, 1707
Aron, M., Père 1217
Artois, Comte d' 654, 655, 1129
Augustus Rex 429 —431
Aureaubert, G., d' 1319
Aynsley China 451, 452

Baehr & Proeschild 82, 1317
Baensch, H. 955, 1086, 1087,
   1111, 1113, 1114

Baignol, E. 1195, 1196
Balbo, G. 697
Balleroy, H. A., Frères 1130
Balleroy, J. & Co. 1131
Bareuther 1698
Barmin Bros 149, 1752 —4
Baroni, G. 1305, 1306, 1309,
   1310
Barr, Flight & Barr 523, 524
Barr, M. 467 —9
Bartholdi, F. 805, 859
Bauer, C. M. & Pfeiffer 1467
Bauscher, A. 383
Bauscher Bros 440, 1700, 1701
Batenin, S. 1750, 1756
Bauer & Pfeiffer 1076, 1077,
   1202, 1206, 1207, 1664
Bayreuther & Co. 488, 514
Beaupoil, marquis de & Co. 1194
Benedikt Bros 528, 1218
Bergdoll, A. 1592
Bernardaux, L. & Co. 1132, 1133
Berthevin, P. 123, 124, 1222 —4
Bettignies family 415
Bettignies, M. 453
Beulé, Reboisson & Parot 1134
Beyerlé, J. L. de 536, 537
Bibra, Heinrich III von 809
Billingsley, W. 17
Billingsley, W. & Coke, J. 1328,
   1329
Billingsley, W. & Walker, S. 1289,
   1290
Bing & Grøndahl 525 —7,
   661 —3, 1031
Birago, L. 1690
Birnay, D. 521
Blancheron, E. 766
Blanka, M. 531

Bloch & Co. 121, 126, 516, 517, 761 —3, 771, 772
Bloch Sept Fontaines 1092 —5, 1097 —9
Bloor, R. 533, 534, 689, 691, 720 —2
"Blue Mist" 1240
"Bohemia" 538, 539
Bohne, E. 477, 799
Bohne, E. & Söhne 1285
Boissonnet, L. 1642
Booth & Coclough Ltd 628 —630, 1216, 1360
Böttger, J. F. 188, 189
Boussemart, J. F. & Delemer 432 —4
Bowker, A. 541, 1559
Brain, E. & Co. 109, 831
Branksome Ceramics 549
Breidenbach, Emmerich von, Kurfürst 290
Bremer & Schmidt 767
Brodel, G. V. 329 —331
Broillet, L. 1078
Brow, Westerheat & Co. 558
Brunswick, Carl I of 790 —3
Buckauer Porzellanmanufaktur 522
Bühl, H. & Söhne 77, 860, 923

Caluve, J. 570
Carasso, painter 333
Carasso, painter 333
Carstens, C. & A. 177, 1702, 1703
Carstens, C. & E. 592, 1385, 1543
"La Cartuja" 1356, 1357, 1389
Cartwright & Edwards Ltd 543, 777, 1659
Catherine the Great 1759 —1761
Cauldon China 571
Ceramica Furga 324, 617
céramique "normande", La 1318
Chamberlain, R. 599, 601
Chamberlains 600, 602 —6
Champion, R. 227 —231, 335, 336, 550
Chang-chia 1888
Chanou, H. F. 598
Chao-ch'in 1904
Chapmans Ltd 1564
Charey, Sauvageau & Hervé 1327

Charles, Duke 1453
Charles III of Spain 129
Chartres, Louis-Philippe, duc de 1189, 1192
Ch'en-kuo 1897
Ch'êng Hua 1810 —3
Chêng Tê 1816, 1817
Ch'en-te the Hermit 1894
Chen T'ien-sui 1900
Ch'en Wen 1893
Chia Ch'ing 1818, 1819,
Chi Ch'ing 1818, 1819, 1842 —5, 1901
Chiang Ming-hao 1903, 1907
Chicaneau, P. 425 —7, 1494, 1554
Ch'ien Lung 1838 —1841
Chin-shih 1892
Ch'ung Chên 1825
Chung family 1896
Coalport China 624 —7
Collingwood Bros Ltd 631
Condé, Prince de 297 —9, 608
Conta & Böhme 77
Cookworthy, W. 337, 475, 476
    Imitations 2054
Copeland, W. T. 632 —9
Copeland, W. T., & Garrett 640 —8
"Cordoba" 866, 867
Cozzi, G. 273, 274
Cretté, L. 556, 665 —8, 1105 —9
Crown Porcelain Co. 130 —2
Crown Staffordshire China 135, 1558, 1560, 1561
Cuccumos, F. 585
Curtis, J. & M. 1188
Custine, A. P. de 577, 580, 581, 622, 623
Custine, A. P. de — Lanfrey, C. F. 1281, 1299 —1301
Cybulski, K. 835, 836
Cyfflé, P. L. 679, 1296, 1597
Czartoryski — Mezer 349, 350

Dahl — Jensens 658
Darte Frères 705, 706
Däuber, F. 419, 421
Davenport 707, 708
De Bey — Chapelle, J. 1582
De Rosly 1374
Delemer 435, 436, 715
Demeuldre, L. — Coché 552 —4

Demeuldre, H. 696
Denton China Company 717
Deruelle, P. 322, 323, 711, 712
Deusch & Co. 306
Dietel, J. 1365
Dihl, J. 731
Dihl, J. & Guerhard 1342
Dillwyn, L. W. 737, 1576—8
Dommer, G. & Co. 420
Donath, P. 738, 1486, 1487,
    1619
Donovan & Son 739—742
Dorez, F. & B. 529
Dornheim, Koch & Fischer
    734—6
Dortu, J. & Müller, F. 114, 115
Doulton & Co. 743—746
Dresden Floral Porcelain Co. 749
Dressel, Kister & Co. 187
Drucko — Lubecki, X. 563
Dubois, J. V. 239, 254
Duesbury, W. 8, 278, 282—5,
    348, 363, 470, 687, 688, 690,
    719, 725, 726, 753, 972, Imita-
    tions 2044
Duesbury, W. & Heath, J.
    681—6
Duesbury, W. & Kean, M. 732,
    733
Dürbeck & Ruckdäschel 1704
Durham China Company 755

Ehwaldt, J. G., Gottbrecht, J. and
    successors 847
Eckert, R. & Co. 264—6, 1673,
    Imitations 2059
Eichler, E. 78, 768, 769
Ekeby Aktiebolag 1627
"Elsa" Porzellan 775
Emanuel, M. & Co. 119, 241,
    255, 307
English paint-room of Chinese and
    European porcelain 515
Ens, K. 778, 779, 1286, 1295,
    1669
"Epiag" 86, 780, 781, 1361
Etablissements Demeuldre 555

Fabrique de Monsieur 1210
Fabrique de Porcelaines Blanches
    & Décorées Anciens Ets. 1155
Fasold & Stauch 133, 1533
Fauquez, J. B. 518, 812, 1488

Fauquez, J. B. & Lamoninary
    816, 1079, 1085
"Favorit" 804
Ferdinand IV Rex 838
Ferdinand VII of Spain 1428
Ferreira Pinto Basto, J. 1638—
    1640, 1665, 1666
Feuillet, J. 798
Fichthorn, J. A. 981
Finney, A. T. & Sons 730
Fischer, A. 391, 392, 1334
Fischer, C. 594, 595, 1588, 1611
Fischer, E. 557
Fischer, F. 813
Fischer & Mieg 178, 827
Fischer & Reichenbach 839
Flight & Barr 709, 823
Flight, Barr & Barr 806, 807, 824
Flight, J. & J. 597, 818—822
Fontanille & Marraud 1135, 1136
Fontebasso, A. & G. 811
Fontebasso Bros 1621—3
Fornari 1655
Frederick Augustus III 803
Fridericus Rex 1393, 1394
Fross Bros 1367
Frye, T. 471,797

Gaignepain, L. F. & Bourgeois, P.
    651—3, 713, 714
Galluba & Hofmann 857, 858
Gardner, F. 845, 846, 1763—8
Gareis, Kühnl & Co. 490—2
"Gefle", Porslin 861, 862
Gerarer Porzellanfabrik 883
Gerold & Co. 1600—2, 1617
Gessner, S. & Spengler, A.
    1719—1721
Geyer, B. R. 125
Geyger, C. 593, 1677, 1678
Giesche 869
Ginori 25, 853, 873—6
Ginori, C. L. 21—4
Ginori, L. 20
Ginori, R. 311
Ginori — Richard 877
Gioanetti, V. A., Dr 332, 727,
    1635, 1636, 1643
Goebel 878
Goebel, W. 19, 120, 1706
Goldschneider, J. 985
Golenichev — Kutuzov, C. 1790
Gorodayu Go Shonzui 1943

242

Gosse, M. F.   508, 510
Gotha, August von   879
Gotzowsky, J. E.   850, 851
Graf & Krippner   1521, 1522
Gräfliche Thun'sche Porzellan-
   fabrik   1606 —1610
Grainger & Co.   885
Grainger, Lee & Co.   886
Greiner & Herda   868
Greiner, F.   814
Greiner, F. C.   55, 56
Greiner, G.   54, 73 —5, 1084,
   1102, 1103, 1127, 1128, 1169
Greiner, G. C.   92, 1584 —7
Greiner, W.   888
Greiner Bros   1396, 1435, 1444,
   1445
Greiner family   1121 —3
Greiner and successors   1649
Grellet Frères   588 —591
Grellet Frères & Massié   828
Gripari, M.   1751
Gronsveldt — Diepenbroek, Count
   225
Grossbaum, M. G.   302
Guérin — Pouyat — Elite
   1138 —1140
Gulyn, J.   1762
Gunther, T. & Co.   1773
Günthersfeld, J. & Co.   79, 852
        Günthersfeld, P.   900
Gutherz, O. & E.   1316
Guy, C. B.   1339, 1347

Haancho, Imitations   2056
Haas & Czjizek   34 —7, 561,
   612 —14, 915, 1505, 1507 —1510
Haas, A.   912 —14, 1504
Hachez, H. & Co.   393
Hachez & Pépin   960
Hadley   917
Haffringue   947
Haidinger, R. E.   439
Haidinger, R. & F.   83, 84
Haidinger Bros   918
Hall Bros Ltd   1418
Hamann, J. W.   1025, 1688
Hamann, J. W. and Greiner, G.
   and J.   1686, 1687
Hammersley & Co.   919, 1186
Hannong, J. A.   89, 901, 902,
   944, 945, 948, 980, 986, 987
Hannong, Paul A.   175, 176, 1350,

1351, 1354, 1355
Hannong, P. A. & La Borde
   952 —4
Hannong, Pierre A.   267, 268,
   903 —5, 1352, 1353
Hansuke   2015
Harstall, Adalbert III, von   810
Hasslacher, B.   403
Haviland, J.   921, 1708
Haviland & Co.   926, 1141, 1142
Haward, R.   906, 920
Heber & Co.
Heber & Co.   925
Hébert, F.   249
Heinrich & Co.   927, 1523 —7
Heintschel, J. E.   984
Henneberg, E.   848, 849, 880
Hering, J. & Sohn   116, 235,
   989, 1037
Hertwig & Co.   102, 1026
Hesse-Darmstadt, Ludwig
   VIII, of   922, 928
Hesse-Kassel, Friedrich II, of
   88, 924
Heubach Bros   5, 69, 312, 908.
   943, 1116
Hewelcke, N. F.   1633, 1634,
   1637
Hildburghausen, W. E., von
   675 —7
Hilditsch & Son   969
Höcke, Friedrich   951
Hoffmann Bros   494
Hohei   2023
Hoju   2022
Hoko or Yoshimitzu   2027
Hollins & Warburton   1294
Holdship, R.   1713
Holm, J. J.   956, 958
Holzapfel & Greiner   1397, 1398
Housel & Guy   1340
Hoyu   2026
Hsien Fêng   1850 —3
Hsuan Tê   1807 —9
Hu — yin, the Taoist   1889
Hudson & Middleton   957
Hughes, E.   946, 1185
Hung Chih   1814, 1815
Hung Wu   1802, 1803
Hutschenreuther   963 —5
Hutschenreuther, C. M.   150, 449,
   450, 620, 961, 1227
Hutschenreuther, C. M., and

successors 962
Hutschenreuther, H. 959, 1332
Hutschenreuther, L. 970, 1118, 1443, 1529
Hüttner & Co. 560, 728, 1036

Illinger & Co. 1364
"Iris" Porcelain 1000, 1001

Jacquemart, J. 1078
Jaeger & Co. 66, 111, 497, 729
Jäger, W. 773, 982, 983
Johnston, D. 542
Jullien, J. & Jacques, S. 272, 338, 532, 546, 547, 1320

Kaestner, F. 815, 1013, 1731
Kaisha (company producing enamel porcelain) 2017
Kampf, R. 1442, 1459
K'ang Hsi 1830 —3
Kanzan 2003
Kato Gosuke 2020
Karlsbader Porzellanfabrik 10017 —1022
Karlskrona Porslinfabrik 1023, 1024
Kato Kanshiro (family of potters) 2013
Kawamoto Masakichi (family of potters) 2014
Kenzan 2004
Kerr & Binns 1027
Kestner & Co. 1028
Khrapunov, N. 1799
Kichiko 1983
Kick, E. 416, 417
Kister, A. W. F. 1055, 1055, 1480
Kisui 1993 —5
Kiyen 1996
Kling & Co. 301
Knaute, B. 246 —8, 530
Knoll, C. 136, 569, 1016
Königliche Hofconditorei Warschau 219, 1029
Kornilov, S. V. 1776
Kosai 1997, 1998
Krantzberger, Mayer & Purkert 1033, 1064, 1693
Krautheim & Adelberg 1062, 1063, 1539
Kretschmann, H. 1012
Kriegel, K. & Co. 1323, 1324

1380 —2
Krippner & Gräf 1521, 1522
Krister Porzellanmanufaktur 38, 1051, 1052, 1057 —9, 1061, 1065, 1070
Kronester, J. & Co. 495
Krug, Fr. 1011
Krüger, E. 1067, 1068
Kuang Hsu 1858 —1861
Kudinov 359
Kuhne, C. 788
Kung Yüan-chi 1899
Kuznetsov 29
Kuznetsov, I. E. 1786, 1787
Kuznetsov, M. S. 1757, 1783 —5, 1788, 1789
Kuznetsov, S. T. 1779 —1782
Kuznetsov, T. I. 1758
Kuznetsov Bros 1777, 1778

La Borde & Hocquart 456
Lahens & Rateau 1193
Lai 1905
Lai-kuan 1910
Lamoninary 1204, 1205
Lanfrey, C. 618, 619
Lang, A. 395
Lang, F. 458, 459, 817
Lang, J. 992
Lange, H. & Co. 1091
Langlois, W. 509
Lanternier, L. & Co. 1143, 1444
Lassia, J. J. 1080 —2
Lauraguais-Brancas, Comte de 472, 1096, 1100, 1101
Lay, J. J. 929
Le Brun, Benoist 1075, 1104, 1191
Leboeuf, A. M. 365
Lehmann, C. A. & Sohn 1115
Lehnert, F. 870, 871
Lenck family 1083
Lenz, J. F. 1726, 1730
Leperre-Durot 117, 118, 1072 —4, 1120
Li Chên-fa 1908
Li-chih 1912
Liang-chi 1906
Liebmann, E. 1478, 1479
Lippert, J. & Haas, A. 1117, 1165, 1166, 1503, 1506
Lippert, J. J. & Haas, V. 1472 —4
Littler, W. 364, 1684, 1717, 1718

244

Locker & Co. 723
Lorenz, V. W. 694, 698, 701, 702
Lormello, G. 1203
Lourioux, L. 830, 840, 1184
Lozelet, M. 1197
Lubieński, H., Count 1198—1200
Lung Ch'ing 1820, 1821
Luso Espanola de Porcelanas,
    Fabrica de Bidosa 1345
Lynker, J. F. & A. 103—106

Macheleid, G. H. 374, 1209
Maier & Co. 770, 1372
Makuzu Kozan 2005
Manka, F. 300
Mann & Porzelius A. G. 95
Manufacture de la Reine Marie
    Antoinette 381, 382
Manufacture du duc d'Angoulême
    855, 856, 1341
Manufacture du duc d'Orléans
    1363, 1246
Manufacture Oude Loosdrecht
    1251, 1258
Manufacture du Prince de Galles
    1377
Manufacture de Porcelaines Ets.
    Legrand 1168
Manufaktur Porselein Mosa 1268
Manufacture Royale de porcelayne
    d'Orléans 238
Marseille, A. 413, 414
Martin, C. & Duché 1147, 1148
Martin Bros 1233
Mathes & Ebel 1219—1221
Mayer, F. J. 1589, 1590
Medici, Francesco II 1208
"Medici" porcelain 325
Meiho 2009
Mérault & Petion 1038, 1039,
    1325
Merlin-Lemas 1149
Metzel Bros 1232, 1234
Metzler Bros & Ortloff 308, 1245,
    1260, 1261
Meyer, S. P. 513, 1269
Mezer, F. 161,2—6, 1748, 1749,
    1774, 1775
Mezer, M. 30, 460, 461,
    478—485, 1009, 1010, 1040—4
Mezer Bros 281
"Mignon" 41, 43, 44
Miklaszewski, A. 1271, 1671,

1712, 1743, 1798
Milde, Ary de 305, 447, 1237
Minton & Boyle 699
Minton, T. 1214, 1215
    Imitations 2055
Minton, T., and successors 1238,
    1239
Mintons & Hollins 826, 1420
Mintons Ltd 607
Mladenof G. & Co. 540
Möhling, J. 366, 394, 411, 412
Moitte, J. 993, 1211, 1212, 1259
Mol, J. de 1248—1250, 1252—7
Möller & Dippe 1631
Mollert, A. 438
Monier, J. B. & Pellevé, D. 1265,
    1266
Montagne, M. 1481
Morgenroth & Co. 881
Mühlhauser, J. P. 864, 865
Müller & Co. 1270, 1733
Müller, E. & A. 664, 1213, 1574
Müller, F. H. 341
Müller, J. N. 995
Müller, P. 498, 804, 1528, 1530,
    1545

Nassau - Saarbrücken, Prince of
    1314, 1315
Nassonov, D. 907, 1792
Nast, J. N. H. 1291, 1292, 1343
Nathusius 1283, 1284
Neuberg, W., von 872, 1297,
    1298
Neukirchner, F. 1696
Neuerer K. G. 1373
New Hall China Factory 1282
Nicolas II. 1791
Nilson, J. O. 916
Nonne, C. 222, 260—3, 973,
    974
Nonne, C. & Roesch, K. 245,
    1313
Novoi Bros 1793
Nowotny, A. 404, 407, 422, 423,
    1312, 1392, 1446, 1447

Oest. Keramik A. G. 81, 108
Ogari Shuhei· 2001
Ohme, H. 61
Orléans, Louis Philippe, duc d'
    1190
Outrequin, J. B. 1246

Pai-shih 1902
Palme, J. 1335—7, 1544
Paragon China Ltd 28, 1338
Paszoa, J. J. 1090
Paul I 1794, 1795
Paulus, J. J. — Greiner, L. 1470, 1471
Pellevé, D. 765, 789, 1330
Perreira, J. M. 1167
Peterinck, F. J. 234, 315—321
Petion 1326, 1362
Petit, Jacob 994
Pfalz, Carl Theodor von der 1591, 1593, 1594
Pfalz-Zweibrücken, Christian IV of 1735
Pfalzer, Z. 151
Pfeffer, E. 882, 884, 1348
Pfeiffer & Löwenstein 678, 1369, 1370, 1387, 1511
Pillivuyt, C. H. 1358, 1359
Pillivuyt & Co. 1230
Pillivuyt family 829
Planché, A. 718
Plant, R. H. & Co. 1368
Pohl Bros 1331, 1415
Poole, T. & Gladstone 1563
Popov, A. 1744, 1745, 1796, 1797
Porcelaine de Casseaux 1572, 1573
porcelaine limousine, La 1145, 1146
Portheim, Porges von 1672
Portheim & Sohn 1383
Porzelius, A. 428
Porzelius & Mann A. G. 95
Porzellanfabrik "Alp" 1201
Porzellanfabrik Günthersfeld A. G. 1349
Porzellanfabrik Kalk G. m. b. H. 240
Porzellanfabrik Victoria A. G. 863, 1656, 1657; Imitations 2061
Potter, C. 544, 1377
Potter, C. & Blancheron 1344
Pouyat, J. 259, 997, 1126
Prahl, A. F.'s widow 143, 144
Prause, F. 834
Putney & Co. 551

Radford, S., Ltd 1416, 1417, 1465

Raised Anchor Period 286
Raynaud & Co. 1151, 1152
Recum, J. N., van 1424, 1674
Recum, P., van 1388, 1395
Regout, L. & Zonen 1263
Reinecke, F. A. 764, 1429
Reinecke, O. 501, 1264, 1371, 1658
Reinholdt & Schlegelmilch 782
Reinl, H. 966, 967
Retsch & Co. 62, 63, 499
Revol, G., Père & Fils 1409, 1410, 1632
Rheinische Porzellanfabrik 909, 1460
"Rhenania" 695, 756
Riber, J. & Co. Imitations 2057
Richard, A. 437
Richard, G. 1404—8, 1431—4, 1436—1440, 1468, 1520
Richard-Ginori 877
Richard G. & Co. 1005
Richard, S. 1236
Richter, Falke & Hahn 1425—7
Richter, J. & Co. 1531
Ridgeway, J. & W. 975, 1441, 1660
Rieber, J. 1411, 1412
Riemann, A. 649
Riessner & Kessel 6, 367, 418 Imitations 2060
Riva, L., de la & Co. 1492
Robert, J. G. 1401, 1402
Robinson & Son 832
Rokubei 1986
Römer & Födisch 800, 801
Rose, J. 64
Rose, J. & Co. 1448
Rosenthal, A. & Co. 441
Rosenthal, A. G. 1419, 1449, 1451
Rosenthal, P. & Co. 748, 1450
Rosetti, G. G. 1421, 1466
Rothberg, W., von 1399
Rousset & Guillerot 1153
Royal Albert Bone China 396, 397
Royal Crown Porcelain Co. 1110
Royal Rockingham Works 93
Royal Staffordshire China 1562
Royal Worcester Porcelain Co. 134
Rulikowski, W. 1769—1772

Russinger, L. 257, 258

Safronov 1755
Sahei 2002
Salisbury China 1489
Salopian China 1491
Salopian Warehouse 1490
San Cristoforo 80, 596
Schachtel, J. 59, 1003, 1004
Schackert Bros 462, 486
Schaller, O. & Co. 279, 280,
    502, 503, 1495, 1496
Schaller, O. & Co. and successors
    785 —7
Schaubach, H. 968, 1499, 1692
Schierholz, C. G. & Sohn 70 —2,
    342 —4
Schlegelmilch, E. 107, 1461,
    1462, 1569 —1571
Schlegelmilch, O. 127, 1030,
    1089, 1512, 1541
Schlegelmilch, R. 1463, 1464,
    1605
Schmerzer & Gericke 303
Schmider, G. 1722, 1727 —9
Schmidt, A. 1032
Schmidt, H. 236, 837, 1378, 1534
Schmidt, J. J. 1630
Schneider, J. & Co. 1119
Schoenau Bros 910, 911, 949,
    950, 971
Schoenau Bros, Swaine & Co.
    269, 1519, 1575
Schomburg, H. & Söhne 1452
Schultz, C., Gabel & Brehm 1400
Schultz, C. & Co. 1430
Schuman, M. & Sohn 1247
Schumann, C. 386, 489, 1497,
    1516
Schumann & Schreider 1498,
    1517, 1580, 1581
Schwaig, A. 1518, 1689, 1705
Seifu 1999, 2000
Séguin 237
Seikozan 2024
Seltmann, C. 783, 784, 1002,
    1711
Seltmann, J. 1667, 1668, 1670
Shang-su 1895
Shaw, J. & Sons 1583
Shelley Potteries 1535
Sheng-kao 1901
Shiozo 1973

Shonzui Gorodayu 1944
Shore & Coggins Ltd 519, 520,
    1391
Shun Chih 1826 —9
Simson Bros 1482
Società Ceramica Italiana 1651,
    1652
Société porcelainière de Limoges
    1154
Soelcher 1514
Sommer & Matschak 1540
Souroux 58, 1475, 1476
Spode, J. 1547 —1552
Sprimont — Fawkener · 275 —7
Sprimont, N. & Gouyn, C. 53,
    256, 611; Imitations 2045
Springer & Co. 85
Staatliche Porzellanmanufaktur
    Berlin 1485
Steinmann, K., G. m. b. H. 1069,
    1538
Sten, H. 347
Sten, H. and Dortu, J. 1225
Stevenson & Handcock 692
Stevenson, Sharp & Co. 724
Stockhardt & Schmidt-Eckert
    1066, 1553
Stone, Coquerel & Legros 1555
Straus, L. & Söhne 1579
Swaine & Co. 1483

Tao Kuang 1846 —9
Taylor, W. 1625
"Terre de Lorraine" 1597
Tharaud, C. 1603
Thieme, C. 68, 122, 671, 673, 751,
    1375, 1376, 1384, 1618, 1626
Thomas & Co. 511, 512, 1542
Thomas, F. 1604
Tielsch, C. 137, 408, 409, 410,
    670, 672, 674, 1596
T'ien Ch'i 1824, 1892
Touze, Lemaître Frères & Blancher
    1156
Trentham Bone China 1620
Triangle period 256, 351, 352
Trou, G. & H. 1515
T'ung Chih 1854 —7
Tuppack, C. H. 1567
Turner, T. 13 —16, 559, 1477,
    1491; Imitations 2046 —2052

Unger, A. 309

247

Unger & Schilde   1413
Unger & Schilde and successors
  1414
Unger, Schneider, Hutschen-
  reuther & Co.   250—3
Union Céramique   1157, 1158
Union Limousine   1159, 1160
Urfus, F.   1628
Utzschneider & Co.   152, 153,
  1568

Vanier, M.   1641
Vaume, J. S.   473, 474
Vermonet, J. & Fils   463—6
Verneuilh & Alluaud   545
Verneuilh, P. & J.   1679, 1680
Vezzi, F. & G.   1644—8, 1650
Vignaud, A.   1161, 1163
Viking Pottery Co.   1661, 1662
Villegoureix   1162, 1164
Villeroy, Duc de   757—760
Villers Cotterets   1663
Voigt Bros   339, 345, 1484
Voigt, H.   67

Wagner & Apel   1694
Wagner, H.   1315
Wahliss, E.   154, 1695
Wan li   1822, 1823
Wanderer, A. C., painter   385
Wang Ping-jun   1913
Wang Shou-ming   1890

Wang Tso-t'ing   1909
"Walküre"   513
Wall, J., Dr   9—11, 232, 243,
  353—8, 796, 1681—3
Walter, C. & Co.   1556, 1557
Weatherly & Crowther   242, 244
Weber, M.   96—8, 1006, 1008
Wegely, W. C.   1676
Wehinger, H. & Co.   1691
Weiss, Kühnert & Co.   887
Widera, Dr & Co.   1231
Wilhelmus Rex   1716
Winterling Bros   500
Winterling, H.   493, 504
Wohlfinger, R.   1699, 1714
Württemberg, Carl Eugen of   100,
  101, 578, 579, 582—4
Württemberg, Ludwig Eugen, of
  1071, 1088

Yü — chai   1911
Yüan Hsin-hsing   1898
Yung Chêng   1834—7
Yung Lo   1804—6
Yusupov, Prince   1746, 1747

Zdekauer, M.   60, 304, 405, 406,
  442, 454, 680, 1734
Zeh, Scherzer & Co   39, 159, 160,
  505—7, 1723—5, 1736
Zeidler, J. & Co.   1732
Zsolnay   326—8, 1737, 1738

INDEX OF PLACES

Aich (Doubí), CZ   366, 394, 411, 412, 457, 780
Alcora, E   360—2
Altenburg, D   401
Alt-Haldensleben, D   303, 1283, 1284
Alt-Rohlau (Stará Role), CZ   60, 300, 304, 403—7, 422, 423, 442, 454, 680, 781, 863, 1119, 1312, 1316, 1392, 1446, 1447, 1656, 1657, 1734
   Imitations 2061
Amberg, D   416, 417
Amstel, NL   419—21
Ansbach, D   112, 113, 161—3, 368—73, 375—80
   Imitations 2058
Arita (Hizen province), J   1943—1957
Arkhangelskoe, RUS   1746, 1747
Arnstadt, D   270, 271
Arras, F   432—6, 715
Arzberg, D   386, 448—50, 489, 1497, 1516
Augarten see Vienna

Baden-Baden, D   151
Bakhteevo, RUS   1742
Baranovka, UA   281, 460, 461, 478—85, 1748, 1749, 1751
Barcelona, E   110
Basdorf, D   462, 486
Bayreuth, D   385, 513, 981, 1269
Bayswater, GB   515
Belleek, IRL   521
Berlin, D   179—86, 340, 850, 851, 1050, 1053, 1054, 1060, 1675, 1676

Berlin, Moabit, D   1247
Blankenhain, D   177, 1067, 1068, 1702, 1703
Bock-Wallendorf, D   133, 1533
Boisette, F   463—6
Bordeaux, F   542, 545, 1193, 1641, 1679, 1680
Boulogne, F   947
Bourg la Reine, F   338, 532, 546, 547, 1320
Bournemouth, GB   549
Bow, GB   8, 242, 244, 278, 282—285, 348, 363, 470, 471, 797, 844, 972
   Imitations 2040, 2041
Božičany see Poschetzau
Březová see Pirkenhammer
Bristol, GB   227—31, 335, 336, 475, 476, 550, 551
Brussels, B   473, 556, 665—8, 1105—9
Brussels, Etterbeek, B   552—5, 696, 788
Brussels, Schaerbeek, B   474
Budapest, H   557, 1737, 1738
Budau (Budov), CZ   395, 458, 459, 817
Budov see Budau
Budy, UA   1757, 1788
Buen Retiro, E   47, 49—52, 129
Burslem, GB   743—6
Bystřice see Wistritz

Caen, F   567, 568
Canetto sull'Oglio see Mantua
Capodimonte, GB   40, 45, 46, 48
Caughley, GB   13—16, 1477, 1491
   Imitations 2046—52

Chantilly, F 297—9, 608, 1217, 1663
Charlottenbrunn (Zofiówka), PL 59, 1003, 1004
Chatillon, F 609, 610
Chelsea, GB 53, 224, 256, 275—277, 286, 351, 352, 611, 1288
Imitations 2045
Chodau (Chodov), CZ 37, 560, 561, 612—14, 728, 1036, 1383, 1425—7, 1672
Chodov see Chodau
Chodzież, PL 562, 615, 616
Cluj see Klausenburg
Ćmielów, PL 563, 621, 656, 835, 836
Coalbrookdale see Coalport
Coalport (Coalbrookdale), GB 64, 572—6, 587, 624—7, 669, 700, 710, 1183, 1293, 1448, 1625
Cobridge, GB 1661, 1662
Coburg, D 649
Copenhagen, DK 18, 31—3, 139—41, 341, 438, 525—7, 657—663, 704, 716, 802, 956, 958, 1031
Creidlitz, D 650, 1346
Crépy en Valois, F 651—3, 713, 714

Dallwitz (Dalovice), CZ 694, 698, 701, 702, 813, 842, 1628
Dalovice see Dallwitz
Damm, D 292—6, 703
Delft, NL 305, 447, 570, 1237
Derby, GB 130—2, 233, 533, 534, 681—92, 718—26, 732, 733, 753, 1110
Imitations 2042—4
Doccia, I 20—5, 311, 853, 873—6, 1278, 1434
Doubí see Aich
Dresden, D 693, 750, 752
Dubí see Eichwald
Dublin, IRL 739—42
Duchcov see Dux
Duisdorf, D 695, 756
Dulevo, UA 1779—82
Dux (Duchcov), CZ 78, 768, 769

Eichwald (Dubí), CZ 121, 126, 516, 517, 761—3, 771, 772, 1231

Eisenberg, D 240, 764, 767, 773, 982, 983, 1015, 1045, 1429
Elbogen (Loket), CZ 83—6, 439, 918, 1012
Elgersburg, D 384, 774, 1226, 1707
Ellwangen, D 143, 144
Erbendorf, D 783, 784
Erkersreuth, D 494
Etiolles, F 765, 789, 1265, 1266, 1330

Fenton, GB 109, 135, 541, 831, 832, 946, 1185, 1416, 1417, 1465, 1558—61
Fischern (Rybáře), CZ 136, 569, 1016—1022
Florence, I 325, 1208
Foëcy, F 829, 830, 840, 1184, 1358
Fontainebleau, F 994
Frankenthal, D 89, 175, 176, 980, 986, 987, 1354, 1355, 1388, 1395, 1424, 1591—4, 1674
Fraureuth, D 800, 801, 833, 841, 1493
Freiwaldau (Gozdnica), PL 236, 837, 1378, 1534
Friedland (Frýdlant), CZ 984
Fryazino, RUS 149, 1752—4
Frýdlant see Friedland
Fulda, D 334, 809, 810
Fürstenberg, D 94, 790—5

Gateshead, GB 755
Gehren, D 79, 852, 900, 1349
Geneva, CH 864, 864
Gera, D 847
Gerona, E 866, 867
Giesshübel (Kysibl, Kyselka), CZ 245—8, 530, 870—2, 1297, 1298
Gorbunovo see Moscow
Gorodnitza (Horodnica), PL 1769—72
Gotha, D 848, 849, 879—82, 884, 1348, 1399, 1400, 1430, 1482
Gozdnica see Freiwaldau
Gräfenroda, D 734—6
Gräfenthal, D 250—3, 887
Grossbreitenbach, D 73, 77, 860, 923
Grünlas (Loučky), CZ 1442, 1459
Grünstadt, D 805, 859

Gustavsberg, S   424, 889—99
Gutenbrunn *see* Zweibrücken

Hackefors, S   916
Hague, The, NL   103—6
Hanley, GB   628—30, 1216, 1240,
   1360
Helsinki, FIN   145, 158, 443—6,
   931, 932, 1333
Herend, H   91, 146—8, 933—42
Hildesheim, D   128
Himeji (Harima province), J
   1980, 1981
Hirado (Hizen province), J   1958,
   1959
Hlubany *see* Lubau
Höchst, D   287—90
Hof Moschendorf, D   501, 1264,
   1371, 1658
Hohenberg, D   150, 620, 961—5,
   1227
Horn (Hory), CZ   1691
Horodnica *see* Gorodnitza
Hory *see* Horn
Hüttensteinach, D   910, 911,
   949, 950, 971

Ilmenau, D   75, 308, 391, 392, 857,
   858, 973, 974, 976—9, 990, 991,
   996, 998, 999, 1245, 1260, 1261,
   1313, 1334, 1649
Irún, E   1345

Jaworzyna Śląska *see* Königszelt
Jedlina Zdrój *see* Charlottenbrunn

Kahla, D   142, 1014, 1115
Kaltenhof (Oblanov), CZ   1365
Kameyama (Hizen province), J
   1961
Karlskrona, S   1023
Kassel, D   88, 924
Katzhütte, D   102, 1025, 1026
Kelsterbach, D   922, 928—30
Klášterec *see* Klösterle
Klausenburg (Cluj), RO   1000, 1001
Kleneč *see* Klentsch
Klentsch (Kleneč), CZ   1032
Kloster Veilsdorf, D   55, 56,
   675—7
Kloster Vessra, D   1653, 1654
Klösterle (Klášterec), CZ   96—8,
   1006—8, 1606—10

Kobe (Setzu province), J   1984
Königszelt (Jaworzyna Śląska), PL
   441, 1034, 1035, 1536, 1537
Könitz, D   1232, 1234, 1235
Köppelsdorf, D   116, 235, 312,
   989, 1037
Köppelsdorf-Nord, D   269, 413,
   414, 1483, 1519, 1575
Korzec, PL   349, 350, 1009, 1010,
   1038—44, 1325, 1326, 1362,
   1774, 1775
Koto (Omi province), J   2008,
   2009
Kowary *see* Schmiedeberg
Kronach, D   748, 1066, 1450, 1553
Krummennaab, D   1091, 1364
Kusyaev, RUS   1799
Kutani (Kaga province), J
   1962—79
Kyoto (Yamashiro province), J
   1985, 1986, 1993—2006
Kysibl *see* Giesshübel

La Moncloa, E   1228, 1229, 1262,
   1428
Landstuhl, D   1065
Lane End, GB   969
Langewiesen, D   127, 1030, 1089,
   1512, 1541
La Seynie, F   1194—6
Lassay, F   472, 1096, 1100, 1101
Lauf, D   1011
Laveno, I   1651, 1652
Leningrad *see* St Petersburg
Le Nove, I   26, 27, 535, 854,
   1279, 1280, 1302—10
Lettin, D   955, 1086, 1087,
   1111—14
Lichte, D   5, 69, 908, 943,
   1116
Lille, F   117, 118, 529, 1072—4,
   1120
Limbach, D   54, 74, 76, 1084,
   1102, 1103, 1121—3, 1127,
   1128, 1169
Limoges, F   565, 566, 588—91,
   828, 926, 997, 1124—6, 1129—
   1164, 1168, 1572, 1573, 1603
Lippelsdorf, D   1694
Lisbon, P   1090, 1167
Loket *see* Elbogen
Longton, GB   28, 388—390, 396,
   397, 402, 451, 452, 519, 520,

543, 631, 717, 730, 749, 754, 777, 919, 957, 1186, 1338, 1368, 1391, 1418, 1489, 1490, 1535, 1562—5, 1568, 1583, 1620, 1659
Longton Hall, GB 364, 1684, 1717, 1718
Lorch, D 306
Lorient, F 1327
Loučky see Grünlas
Lowestoft, GB 12, 223, 398—400, 906, 920, 1187, 1188, 1685
Lubartów, PL 1198—1200
Lubau (Hlubany), CZ 1233
Lubenz (Žlutice), CZ 966, 967
Ludwigsburg, D 99—101, 578, 579, 582—4, 1071, 1088, 1393, 1394, 1716
Lunéville, F 679, 1296, 1597
Luxembourg, L 1092—5, 1097—9

Maastricht, NL 1263, 1268
Mäbendorf, D 1219—21
Magdeburg-Buckau, D 522
Mannheim, D 909, 1460
Mantua, Canetto sull'Oglio, I 324, 617, 843
Marieberg, S 123, 124, 347, 1222—5
Marktleuthen, D 493, 504
Marktredwitz, D 66, 111, 497, 729, 1604, 1696
Marktschwaben, D 90
Marseille, F 1401, 1402
Mayerhöfen, D 528, 1218
Mehun-sur-Yèvre, F 1230, 1359
Meissen, D 188—221, 429—31, 803, 1029, 1046—9, 1267, 1287, 2032—9
Mennecy, F 757—60
Merkelsgrün (Merklín), CZ 65, 775
Merklín see Merkelsgrün
Middleton, GB 776
Milan, I 80, 437, 596, 877, 1005, 1236, 1404—8, 1431—3, 1436—40, 1468, 1520
Mitterteich, D 119, 241, 255, 307, 496, 1241—3, 1411, 1412, 1531
Imitations 2057
Moabit see Berlin
More, RUS 1790

Moscow, RUS 359, 907, 1773, 1793
Moscow, Gorbunovo, RUS 1744, 1745, 1796, 1797
Moscow, Narotkaya, RUS 1755
Moscow, Ryazan, RUS 1762
Moscow, Spassk, RUS 1792

Nabeshima (Hizen province), J 1960
Nagoya (Ovari province), J 2017, 2018
Nantgarw, GB 1289, 1290
Naples, I 838, 1272—6
Neu-Rohlau (Nová Role), CZ 538, 539
Neustadt, D 925
New Hall see Shelton
Niderviller, F 536, 537, 577, 580, 581, 618, 619, 622, 623, 1281, 1299—1301
Niedersalzbrunn (Szczawienko), PL 61, 834
Nová Role see Neu-Rohlau
Novgorod, RUS 29
Novi Sad, YU 1311
Novokharitino, RUS 1758, 1777, 1778
Nymphenburg, D 170—4
Nyon, CH 114, 115

Oberhohndorf, D 815, 1013, 1731
Oberkotzau, D 868, 1373
Oblanov see Kaltenhof
Oeslau, D 19, 120, 878, 1706
Ohrdruf, D 82, 301, 1028, 1317
Oissel, F 1318
Orléans, F 57, 238, 1075, 1104, 1191, 1319
Osaka (Setsu province), J 1983
Ostrov see Schlackenwerth
Otokoyama (Kii province), J 2007
Ottweiler, D 1314, 1315
Oude Loosdrecht, NL 1248—58
Ovari (Ovari province), J 2010

Paris, Barrière de Reuilly, F 598, 1080—2
Paris, Clignancourt, F 322, 323, 711, 712, 993, 1210—12, 1259

252

Paris, Faubourg Saint Denis, F
267, 268, 654, 655, 905
Paris, Gros Caillou, F 387, 1078
Paris, Pont aux Choux, F 41, 43,
44
Paris, Rue Amelot, F 1190, 1246,
1363
Paris, Rue de Bondy, F 731, 855,
856, 1341, 1342
Paris, Rue de Charonne, F 705,
706
Paris, Rue de Crussol, F 544,
766, 1344, 1377
Paris, Rue du Faubourg Saint
Denis, F 1514
Paris, Rue Fontaine au Roy, F
257—9
Paris, Rue de la Paix, F 798
Paris, Rue du Petit Carrousel, F
1339, 1347
Paris, Rue de la Roquette, F 58,
239, 249, 254, 1475, 1476
Paris, Rue Popincourt, F 1291,
1292, 1343
Paris, Rue Saint Merry, F 1555
Paris, Rue Thiroux, F 365, 381,
382, 1340
Parowa see Tiefenfurth
Passau, D 187, 291, 1083
Pécs, H 326—8
Pinxton, GB 17, 1328, 1329
Pirkenhammer (Březová), CZ
138, 178, 595, 827, 839, 951,
1361
Plankenhammer, D 487, 1367,
1379
Plaue, D 70—2, 342—4
Plymouth, GB 337
Imitations 2054
Podbořany see Podersam
Podersam (Podbořany), CZ 1201
Pontenx, F 1374
Poschetzau (Božičany), CZ 770,
1372
Pössneck, D 87
Potschappel, D 68, 122, 671, 673,
751, 1375, 1376, 1384, 1618,
1626
Prague, CZ 1323, 1324, 1380—2
Probstzella, D 959, 1332

Rantei (Yamashiro province), J
1991, 1992

Rauenstein, D 1396, 1435, 1444,
1445
Rehau, D 39, 159, 160, 505—7,
1723—5, 1736
Reichenstein, D 531
Riga, LV 1783—5
Rockingham, GB 548
Rome, I 585
Rörstrand, S 125, 1403, 1453—8
Imitations 2056
Röslau, D 500
Rosslau, D 1452
Rotschütz, D 1413, 1414
Rozenburg, NL 1469
Rudolstadt, D 477
Rybáře see Fischern

Saargemünd, D 152, 153, 1568
Saint Amand les Eaux, F 415,
453, 518, 812, 1488
Saint Cloud, F 1—3, 42, 425—7,
1494, 1515, 1554
Saint Uze, F 1409, 1410, 1632
Saint Vallier, F 1481, 1642
Sakurai (Setsu province), J 1982
Sampei (Awaji province), J 2021
Sargadelos, E 1492
Satsuma (Satsuma province), J
2022—31
Sceaux, F 272, 1582
Schaala, D 67
Schedewitz, D 309
Scheibe-Alsbach, D 1055, 1056,
1480
Schelten (Šelty), CZ 1335—7,
1544
Schirding, D 7, 1500—2
Schlackenwerth (Ostrov), CZ
678, 1369, 1370, 1387, 1511
Schlaggenwald (Slavkov), CZ
34—6, 912—15, 1117, 1165,
1166, 1470—4, 1503—10,
1540
Schlottenhof, D 1513
Schmiedeberg (Kowary), PL
1331, 1415
Schney, D 1478, 1479
Schönwald, D 995
Schorndorf, D 586, 1076, 1077,
1202, 1206, 1207, 1467, 1664,
1715
Schwarza-Saalbahn, D 664,
1213, 1574

253

Schwarzenbach, D 279, 280, 495, 502, 503, 1495, 1496
Schwarzenhammer, D 1498, 1517, 1580, 1581
Seedorf, D 1733
Selb, D 498, 804, 927, 970, 1062, 1063, 1118, 1419, 1443, 1449, 1451, 1485, 1521—30, 1539, 1545, 1732
Šelty see Schelten
Seto (Ovari province), J 2011—16
Seville, E 1356, 1357, 1389
Sèvres, F 1180—2, 1244, 1277, 1422, 1423, 1532
Shelton, GB 558, 571, 975, 1441, 1660
Shelton, New Hall, GB 1282, 1294
Sitzendorf, D 339, 345, 1484
Sitzerode, D 374
Slavkov see Schlaggenwald
Sophienthal, D 511, 512, 1542
Sorau (Żary), PL 592, 1385, 1543
Spechtsbrunn, D 1546
St Petersburg, RUS 1739—41, 1750, 1756, 1759—61, 1776, 1791, 1794, 1795, 1800, 1801
Stadtlengsfeld, D 310, 313, 787, 808, 1366, 1386
Stanowitz (Strzegom), PL 1556, 1557
Stará Role see Alt Rohlau
Stoke-on-Trent, GB 607, 632—648, 699, 826, 1214, 1215, 1238, 1239, 1420, 1547—52
  Imitations 2055
Strasbourg, F 901—4, 944, 945, 948, 988, 1350—3
Strzegon see Stanowitz
Suhl, D 107, 1461, 1462, 1569—71
Swansea, GB 737, 1556—8
Swinton, GB 93, 548
Szczawienko see Niedersalzbrunn

Tannawa (Ždanov), CZ 1589, 1590
Tettau, D 92, 1584—7, 1598—1602, 1617
Tiefenfurth (Parowa), PL 738, 1069, 1486, 1487, 1538, 1567, 1619

Tillowitz (Tulowice), PL 782, 1463, 1464, 1605
Tirschenreuth, D 155, 156
Togyoku (Mino province), J 2019, 2020
Tomaszów, PL 30, 1612—16
Tournai, B 234, 314—21
Treviso, I 811, 1621—3
Triptis, D 1321, 1322, 1624
Trnovany see Turn
Tulowice see Tillowitz
Turin, I 1421, 1466
Turn (Trnovany), CZ 6, 154, 157, 367, 418, 1695
  Imitations 2060
Tver, RUS 1789

Uhlstädt, D 564, 1629
Ulm, D 1630
Unterköditz, D 1631
Unternhaus, D 883
Unterweissbach, A 95, 428, 968
Uppsala, S 861, 862, 1024, 1627

Valenciennes, F 816, 1079, 1085, 1204, 1205
Valognes—Bayeux, F 508—10
Vaux, F 456
Vendrennes, F 1197
Venice, I 273, 274, 1633, 1634, 1637, 1644—8, 1650
Verbilki, RUS 845, 846, 1763—8
Vienna, A 164—9, 302, 540, 985
Vienna, Augarten, A 455, 1709
Vienna, Wilhelmsburg, A 81, 108, 825, 1710
Vierzon, F 393, 960
Villedieu sur Indre, F 992
Vincennes, F 237, 952—4, 1170—9, 1189, 1192
Vinovo, I 329—33, 697, 727, 1203, 1635, 1636, 1643, 1655
Vische, I 1690
Vista Alegre, P 1638—40, 1665, 1666
Vohenstrauss, D 1002, 1667, 1668, 1670
Volkhov, RUS 1786, 1787
Volkstedt-Rudolstadt, D 4, 222, 260—6, 778, 779, 799, 814, 888, 1209, 1270, 1285, 1286, 1295, 1397, 1398, 1579, 1595, 1669, 1673

254

Imitations 2059
Volokitino, RUS   1271, 1671, 1712, 1743, 1798

Walbrzych *see* Waldenburg
Waldenburg (Walbrzych), PL   38, 137, 408, 410, 670, 672, 674, 1051, 1052, 1057—9, 1061, 1070, 1596
Waldershof, D   921, 1697, 1708
Waldsassen, D   488, 490—2, 514, 1698
Wallendorf, D   1499, 1686—8, 1692
Weesp, NL   225, 226
Weiden, D   383, 440, 1700, 1701, 1711
Weingarten, D   1699, 1714
Weissenstadt, D   1704
Weisswasser, D   1518, 1689, 1705
Wilhelmsburg *see* Vienna
Windisch-Eschenbach, D   785—7
Wistritz (Bystřice), CZ   1033, 1064, 1693

Worcester, GB   9—11, 134, 232, 243, 346, 353—8, 467—9, 523, 524, 597, 599—606, 709, 796, 806, 807, 818—24, 885, 886, 917, 1027, 1681—3, 1713
Imitations 12, 2053
Wunsiedel, D   62, 63, 499
Würzburg, D   593, 1677, 1678

Yeiraku (Yamashiro province), J   1987—90

Żary *see* Sorau
Ždanov *see* Tannawa
Zell-Harmersbach, D   1722, 1726—30
Žlutice *see* Lubenz
Zofiówka *see* Charlottenbrunn
Zürich, CH   1719—21
Zweibrücken, Gutenbrunn, D   1390, 1735
Zwickau, D   594, 1588, 1611